The Tempest and *Hag-Seed*

A Textual Conversations Guide

Kirsten Oakley

For Victoria, whose passion teaching this module will always remain with me. For Beau, who teaches me about the magic of the theatre. And for Lisa, who believes that like Prospero, I can create anything if I just keep writing!

Five Senses Education Pty Ltd
2/195 Prospect Highway,
Seven Hills 2147
NSW Australia

First Published 2023

Oakley, Kirsten
The Tempest and *Hag-Seed* – A Textual Conversations Guide
ISBN 978-1-76032-484-1

Contents

Textual Conversations

What does the module require?

The focus in this module is on the way that studying texts in comparison can reveal resonances or dissonances, or the similarities and differences between the texts. Students look at texts which reimagine or reinvent a text, or an aspect of a text, and consider how the original text has been mirrored or changed in this reframing.

By considering paired texts in this manner, students are able to discuss whether issues, values, assumptions or perspectives from the texts are shared or differing and how they are depicted in each text. Through the comparison of texts, students should be able to discuss the influence of context, values and other texts.

Through a close study of the texts and their textual features and conventions, students analyse and evaluate their texts. This analysis should include the text's purpose, form, style and language concepts like motif, allusion and intertextuality. They consider how their understanding, enjoyment and appreciation of both texts was enhanced through the comparison of texts, and how innovating with language concepts can create new meaning. Students should evaluate and experiment with innovation and language to compose informed and imaginative responses.

The contextual influence of the composer is also an integral element in this module. Students must discuss the personal, social, cultural and historical context that has influenced the composer when creating their text. They should evaluate how this has shaped the perspectives in each text and whether the texts share any common values. They should also consider their own context, how it influences their perception of the text and the effect it has on their writing.

By the conclusion of the module, students should have formed their own personal opinions about the comparative texts.

Studying *The Tempest and Hag-Seed*

For Textual Conversations

If you are studying *The Tempest* and *Hag-Seed*, then you are doing the Textual Conversations Module of the Advanced English Course. The approach that this guide takes is to look at each text separately first. Once you are sure that you have understood each text, you can then compare them properly.

Module A requires students to know and understand the context and influences of each text. That means that you will need to implement research or knowledge from the history of each text, the composer and the time in which it was originally composed. You should consider how the original audience viewed the text, and how the composer's expectations of this audience shaped their work.

The word "conversation" in the title of this unit means that you must be able to discuss the relationship between your texts. This is the way that each text dialogues or relates to the other text. You will find that there is more dialogue with Atwood's text than Shakespeare's text, but this conversation also includes you as responding to the text, so don't forget that you can be a key part of this conversation!

The Textual Conversations module requires you to explore how viewing two texts together allows you to understand them in more depth. You should know what new insight you gained into each by viewing them in tandem. Through this comparison and contrast of the texts you should gain a better understanding of the original values and contexts of each text, and how your own values have influenced the way that you view them.

Connections between the texts can come in many forms. They could be a direct reference to the other text or an indirect reference or allusion to it. These direct references are the explicit references like the intertextuality or allusion that the syllabus discusses, but you can also find implicit references. Additionally, you may find similarities or differences in the values, issues and perspectives reflected in the text. The aspects of the texts may be similar, or they may be the same ideas, structures or features but with a different opinion expressed, or they may be opposing. The structure and techniques of the texts could also be used to establish a connection. Alternatively, the innovative techniques used by the contemporary composer may lead to new ideas and understanding.

For more insight into the connections that can be identified intertextually, you should look at the pages later in this study guide that elaborate specifically on the links between *The Tempest* and *Hag-Seed.* You will also find that connections are explicitly identified for you throughout the Themes, Characters, Setting and the Language Features and Narrative Techniques and other sections of the guide.

Context, Values and Influence

While this module is not solely about context, due to the discrepancy in the dates of production, context of the text becomes an important concept when comparing texts. Context in the module means the social, historical and cultural background of the text. It includes important events that occurred before the text, like recent changes in monarchy or shipwrecks, the social structure of the society, such as the differing roles and status of men and women and typical occupations and interests of the time. It also takes into account cultural elements, like the dominant religion and the current set of beliefs of the time.

The context of the composer is usually directly responsible for their set of values. Each text composed has values inherent in it. This set of values is commonly a direct result of the social, historical and cultural context and can also derive from the composer's personal context. The perspectives evident in the texts reflect the context and assumptions which are evident in the composer's society. Usually, a composer subconsciously reflects the assumptions, values and perspectives of his or her society in their work. Sometimes, they purposefully rebel against these values in order to reflect the issues or problems in their context. The values inherent in the composer's context are therefore an important element when considering the construction of each text.

Consider a narrative you have written yourself previously, perhaps as part of an English lesson or course. You probably unwittingly reflected your own values and assumptions in the characters and plot. Let's suppose the story was about a young, attractive girl who features on a reality show and subsequently becomes famous. You would be reflecting the values of your society that idolises celebrity, youth and beauty. You would in addition be revealing society's obsession with television and current love of the reality genre. Imagine that you have also included a romance in your story. As your society tends to be biased towards showcasing relationships with older men and younger women in mainstream media and movies, it is likely that the relationship was between a slightly older man and a younger woman. It is also probable that you would write about love and attraction as the reason for the union as your society does not pressure women to marry for economic reasons or to gain status. Unless a composer is consciously trying to subvert societal norms, then they compose works that mirror their society's values.

Some composers do set out to ensure that they do not reflect the values of their time. A composer may be affiliated with a different set of values from the norm, for example if they belonged to a cult or an extreme political party. If a composer is deliberately subverting values, then you should have unearthed this in your research into the composer and context and you would need to discuss this in your essays.

There are many examples of texts that reflect the dominant values of their composers and also those of their intended audience. For example, a text that was written in a patriarchal society might reflect this through an emphasis on male characters, revealing that men are valued over women in this time. A text written for a Christian audience might reflect their values through the portrayal of a villain who breaks many of their commandments. The prospect of the audience and their values in this instance would lead the composer to expect that the responders would class the villain as evil. Many texts written in Jacobean times refer to the monarch as God's representative on Earth, reflecting this popular belief and hence one of the values of the time. The texts that you are studying for this module fall into this category. They are created by composers who reflect the dominant values of their audience, but both also question these values to some extent through their portrayal of characters. In this way, Shakespeare and Atwood are similar.

In many texts the protagonist exemplifies the values that the composer wishes to promote. However, both Prospero and Felix are questionable protagonists, who make us question their right to the status and privilege they are given in their society.

Try to ensure that you don't confuse the values of the text with the text's value. The value of the text is the text's worth, and why it is important in this society and in its original context. The notion of textual integrity is part of this concept. Textual integrity is how well the composer has created a unified text using forms and features. The text's worth and value will depend on the textual integrity of the text. A text that has textual integrity will be valued in a range of contexts. You might be asked about textual integrity, the text's value or the values of the text in this unit.

Activities

Try to complete these tasks to ensure that you understand the concepts of context, values and their influence.

- Imagine that you have just seen a novel in which the main character is a legal aid lawyer who is married and regularly attends the gym. Explain what the composer's characterisation reveals about the dominant values of the time.
- Research the context of both of your texts. Once you have done this, use different coloured highlighters to label each contextual point as social, historical or cultural. If you don't have roughly the same amount of points for each aspect, then keep researching.
  (You may wish to read the context sections of this guide and add this to your list.)
- After looking at your contextual research for each text write a set of values for each context. Once you have done this you can start to think about how these values are reflected in each text. (A further extension task is to then link these values to scenes in *The Tempest* and *Hag-Seed* which display these values to the audience. For example, the patriarchal values of the Jacobean period are exemplified through the scene when Prospero reveals his backstory to Miranda, shown in his commands to her, his tone and his enchantment which forces her to sleep.)

Context of *The Tempest*

The Tempest was written by William Shakespeare. It is believed to have been one of his last works. It is thought to have been written in 1610 and 1611. It was first performed for King James and then performed again at the wedding of his daughter Elizabeth.

Shakespeare's inspiration for the play was probably the 1609 shipwreck of the *Sea Venture* in Bermuda, but there were many famous shipwrecks at this time.

The Jacobean Era was a time of great adventure for many of the English people. It was the middle of three centuries of exploration for European sailing vessels, who brought back goods, gold and people from other worlds. The English were thrilled by stories of these adventures and would attend exhibits of artefacts, animals and even people from far away worlds. Reports from John Smith, who had encountered Pocahontas, had been published in 1608 and this famous tale was just one which had captured the imagination of the Jacobean people.

King James believed in expanding the Empire of the British realm and the English did not recognise the traditional native ownership of the lands they sought to inhabit. This attitude is evident in the relationship between Caliban and Prospero, as Caliban's right to the island has been ignored by the Duke. Thus the play reflects the colonial attitudes of the British Empire.

The patriarchal system in Jacobean England is also represented in the play. The last male monarch before James, Henry VIII, had desperately wanted a son, as previously only men had been recognised as monarchs on the English throne. The monarch between Henry VIII and James, Queen Elizabeth was renowned for both her intelligence and skill with languages. Her father Henry VIII was reportedly extremely proud of her many achievements. Yet despite this, Henry used annulments, executions and divorces to change wives and try to legitimise his son instead of his daughters as this society valued men over women. This was after all, a society in which girls could not attend school and in which women were not supposed to own property. Marriage in this environment was the only way a typical woman could gain status. Elizabeth never married and was known as the Virgin Queen until her death. James was a second cousin, once removed who had gained Elizabeth's favour to be named heir and had previously been on Scotland's throne.

King James I was a Presbyterian, but the balance of power lay with the Protestants in the court. James faced opposition from Catholics who believed that they were not represented by the crown. James had not opposed Queen Elizabeth's execution of Mary, Queen of Scots, (his mother) the last strong Catholic hopeful for the throne. He had also successfully thwarted the Gunpowder Plot, which was a threat to his throne by Catholic dissenters. This was a salient reminder to Shakespeare's audience of the tensions between Catholics and Protestants. Thus, the audience would have an excellent understanding of the sort of political betrayal and rebellions featured in *The Tempest*.

There were other divisions in Jacobean society. It had a fairly strict class system with peasants and servants in the lowest classes. The royals and the nobles were the highest class and due respect was usually paid to them in Shakespearean drama through the formal language and iambic pentameter in which they spoke. Any servants who were represented spoke in course, crude prose. Audiences obviously accepted this representation as accurate, as all classes loved the theatre and would attend performances. The different future offered for Caliban, Stephano and Trinculo shows that they are not given the same treatment as the nobles in this society.

Briefly, theatres had been banned from London due to the spread of the plague. There was also a movement of Puritans who sought to outlaw theatres and had been briefly successful when James was King. But in general, Jacobeans loved plays and companies and theatres thrived. The growth of the theatre was helped by the fact that royalty loved the art, and many plays were staged specifically for the court. Shakespeare's core players at this time were called "The King's Men." The metatheatre and elements of the masque in the play reference the audience's love of theatre and their familiarity with it as the most popular art form of the time.

The Puritan movement mentioned earlier had briefly flourished under Queen Elizabeth. Puritans were essentially severe Protestants and they had hoped that the past queen would promote their extreme views. After all, it was the influence of Elizabeth and her brother Edward that had really established the Protestant religion that their father had begun. Puritans believed that people were predestined for heaven and that little free will was involved. When Elizabeth condemned the public debates of the Puritans, she essentially encouraged people to dismiss their teachings. It is not surprising that many philosophers of the time then started to speculate about whether all events and circumstances were fate or God's will or whether an individual had a measure of free will and an influence over their own lives. This questioning of fate, destiny and free will is evident in the play.

Despite the power of the Church and the attraction towards religion, people of the Jacobean Age were remarkably superstitious. They believed in ghosts and curses and thought that the Devil had given special powers to people who had embraced him. They also believed in witches and would believe that Sycorax was a witch who had literally imprisoned Ariel. King James himself had written a book on witchcraft and demons, which was widely read. Other superstitions they wholeheartedly embraced included the belief that the weather reflected the events that were occurring and that storms were bad omens.

As with many English monarchs, there were many plots against King James. One notable plot was the Gunpowder plot, where Guy Fawkes had planned to blow up Parliament House with gunpowder. Political intrigue was therefore a relevant theme that appeared in many dramatic plays. People at this time also believed in the Divine Right of Kings. This means that they believed that the monarch was placed on the throne by God and was supposed to be his representative on Earth. Any disruption to God's plans for the throne was thought to cause chaos in the world order.

A publication that had affected the way that learned people looked at those in power was *The Prince* written earlier that century by Niccolo Machiavelli. This work asserted that to survive and become powerful, rulers would have to eschew their morals and only operate in their own interests. Charisma and oratory skill were asserted as better virtues for leaders than strong morals and religious ideals. Audiences watching Shakespeare's portrayal of *The Tempest* would question whether Prospero or his brother was a better Duke.

This was, of course, not the only work that had affected Shakespeare's audience. The Renaissance had begun in the 14th Century and continued until the 17th Century. It was just reaching England in Shakespeare's time, and thus he, along with Milton and Marlowe, were seen as some of the great writers of the Renaissance. The Renaissance also encompassed great developments in art, education and philosophy. The philosophy of the Renaissance was essentially humanism. Humanists believed that men were important as they had developed the world that God had given them. They also thought that beauty of all forms was important as it represented worth, and could be a path to God. The Renaissance had also influenced the way that people viewed history, and a learning and reworking of classical sources became fashionable.

The influence of Thomas More's *Utopia* has been noted in *The Tempest*. Both Prospero and Gonzalo have a vision for the island which fits their concept of utopia.

It is important to remember that despite the divisions between religions and philosophies in Jacobean England, the principles of the movements remained the same. Nearly all people believed in the Bible and what it taught, and thus their values were similar. Christian values included loyalty to God and the family, honesty, humility, fidelity and forgiveness. Thus, Prospero essentially finds redemption with the audience by giving up the black arts and forgiving his enemies, aligning himself with the dominant Jacobean values.

Activities

- Find three events in the play which reflect the events that would be familiar to the audience in Jacobean England.
- Write a paragraph about Shakespeare's characterisation of Prospero. You must include the phrase, "Jacobeans would view the fact that Prospero had redeemed himself..." Ensure that you refer to specific contextual details in your answer.

Summary of *The Tempest*

Act I, Scene i

- The play begins with the noise of thunder, signalling a tempest, or storm. The crew is seen panicking about the danger that they may be in, as their boat is close to land and may run aground. The Master, or captain, orders the Boatswain to quickly act to stop this happening.
- The nobles appear from below decks and want to know what is happening. The Boatswain tries to order them below so he can work. Gonzalo, the king's advisor is disgusted at the treatment they are receiving and vows that the Boatswain will live so that he can hang him for his insolence.
- Eventually the nobles realise the severity of the situation and retire below to pray.
- Voices from offstage are heard saying that the ship is splitting and saying goodbye to their loved ones.

Quote

"What cares these roarers for the name of the king?"

(Boatswain about the threatening waves) I, i, 16

Act I, Scene ii

- This scene (and the rest of the play) is set on a remote, largely deserted island. Miranda, the young daughter of Prospero, asks him if he is responsible for the storm. This immediately helps the audience to recognise that he has magical powers. She pleads with him for the lives of the people she has heard suffering on the boat. He tells her that no one was hurt and asks her to help remove his magic cloak.
- Prospero decides to tell Miranda the story of how they came to be on the island. He was once the Duke of Milan, and they lived a life of nobility in Italy. Prospero became interested in magic and spent

time studying his books on the dark arts and began neglecting his duties. His brother Antonio started to perform his duties for him and manage the state of Milan. Antonio wanted Prospero's title, so he agreed to pay an annual sum to the King of Naples in return for his help usurping his brother. They take Prospero and the three-year-old Miranda to a rickety boat and put them out to sea to perish.

- Miranda is shocked by the story and doesn't understand how they made it to the island. Prospero reveals that a kind man named Gonzalo hid food, water and Prospero's magic books in the boat so they would survive.
- Prospero reveals that the enemies who betrayed him are now shipwrecked on the island. He then uses his magic to make his daughter sleep.
- Ariel is called forth by Prospero. Ariel reveals that he is a spirit who can fly and dive into fire. He has followed Prospero's orders and has used his magic to make it look like the nobles' ship is on fire. He reports that they were convinced that they were in danger, and all leapt into the water with Ferdinand leaping first.
- Prospero checks that all the nobles were unharmed and that they made it safely to shore, and Ariel confirms that they did.
- Ariel reminds Prospero that he promised to free him. Prospero reminds him that years ago he freed him from the twisted pine tree that the witch Sycorax had imprisoned him in. When Prospero first came to the island, Sycorax had died, leaving only her son Caliban and Ariel had been left trapped in the tree for twelve years. Prospero threatens to use his magic to imprison Ariel in an oak if he doesn't obey him.
- Prospero wakes Miranda and calls Caliban, who refuses to come. Prospero tells him that spirits will punish him tonight.
- Miranda is dismissive and insulting to Caliban when he appears. In their dialogue on stage the audience learns that Prospero initially treated Caliban like a son, but then Caliban tried to rape Miranda as he wanted to start a family. After this he has been punished and treated like a slave. Caliban leaves, angry that he must obey.

- Ariel, who is invisible to everyone on stage except Prospero, enters playing music and singing. He leads Ferdinand with his music, who is grieving his father, whom he believes has drowned.
- Miranda and Ferdinand see each other and are immediately attracted to each other, using hyperbolic language to describe the other person.
- Wanting to ensure that the attraction lasts, Prospero decides to put some obstacles in the path of their love. He uses his magic to arrest Ferdinand, charging him as a spy. Miranda is shocked by her father's actions.

Quote

> "This island's mine by Sycorax my mother,
> Which thou tak'st from me."
>
> (Caliban to Prospero) I, ii, 331

Questions for Act I

1. How does Shakespeare establish Prospero's power in this act?
2. How would contemporary audiences view Caliban's treatment?
3. Why has Prospero led Ferdinand to their cell (their residence)?

Act II, Scene i

- The nobles are seen washed up, unharmed on a different part of the island. Alonso is grieving because he believes that Ferdinand is drowned. Gonzalo attempts make the King feel better, but Alonso does not want to be cheered up.
- Antonio and Sebastian make fun of Gonzalo. They often do this in asides and bets, but will also openly mock him.
- Gonzalo sees the utopic qualities of the isle and the bounteous potential it has. He references the fact that they were all travelling from the marriage of the King's daughter Claribel in Tunisia. Gonzalo tries to give Claribel a compliment by comparing her to the mythical figure Dido, but he gets the story wrong.

- Francisco, another lord, mentions that there is hope for Ferdinand as he saw him strongly swim away. Alonso dismisses this as he believes he is dead.
- Gonzalo gives a speech about how they could start a new commonwealth on this island with no rulers, education, laws, status or trade. Sebastian and Antonio point out all the reasons why this wouldn't work.
- Ariel arrives, invisible to the men but not to the audience. He plays music which makes everyone but Sebastian and Antonio sleep.
- Antonio tells Sebastian that he should be the King of Naples and that now Ferdinand is dead, all they would have to do would be to kill Alonso and he would inherit the crown.
- Sebastian is reluctant, but Antonio reminds him that he stole the title from his brother Prospero. He states that Claribel is too far away to run Naples and that no one will know what happens in the island. They agree that they will have to kill Gonzalo as well, as he will never allow Sebastian to take charge, but they believe the rest of the nobles will fall in line.
- Sebastian and Antonia draw their swords ready to kill Alonso and Gonzalo in their sleep. Ariel enters as Prospero has seen that Gonzalo is in danger. He whispers in Gonzalo's ear to wake him and he does, waking the king as well.
- Sebastian and Antonio are discovered with their swords drawn. They state that they heard lions and were protecting the King.

Questions for Act II, Scene i

1. What different personalities have you observed amongst the nobles?
2. Why does Prospero save Gonzalo?

Quotes

"No occupation, all men idle, all;
And women too, but innocent and pure;"
(Gonzalo's vision for the isle) I, i, 151–152

"Whereof what's past is prologue; what to come
In yours and my discharge."

(Antonio) II, i, 249–250

Act II, Scene ii

- A storm is heard as Caliban is gathering wood. He delivers a soliloquy about how Prospero's spirits make him suffer when he is not obedient.
- Caliban sees Trinculo, the jester coming and thinks he is a spirit, so he hides under a cloak.
- Trinculo does not understand what Caliban is, but wishes he was able to exhibit him in England as he knows he would make money from people viewing the spectacle. As the storm starts, he decides to hide under the cloak with Caliban.
- Stephano, a drunk butler appears, singing a dirty song. He thinks that the cloak is a four-legged monster, especially when Caliban begins begging the spirits not to hurt him.
- Stephano decides to give the monster some alcohol and finds Caliban's head. At first, he spits it out, but then he starts to drink.
- Seeing Trinculo's legs, Stephano pulls his friend out. They celebrate the fact that the butler came ashore by clinging to barrels of wine, which he now has access to. Caliban is also excited by their access to this alcohol.
- Caliban swears to serve Stephano as his new master and kisses the bottle to seal his promise. Trinculo is doubtful of his loyalty. Caliban promises to show them the secrets of the island.

Questions for Act II, Scene ii

1. What comment is being made in this act about the treatment of people in colonised lands?
2. What parody of both the lower class and imperialism is being offered? How would it be viewed differently by Jacobeans and by contemporary audiences?

Quotes

> "For every trifle are they set upon me,
> Sometime like apes, that mow and chatter at me
> And after bite me."
>
> (Caliban about Prospero's spirits) II, ii, 8–10

> "A strange fish. Were I in England now — as once I was — and had but this fish painted, not a holiday fool there but would give a piece of silver."
>
> (Trinculo about Caliban) II, ii, 25–27

ACT III Scene i

- Ferdinand is seen performing manual labour. He tells the audience that he doesn't mind suffering because he can see Miranda and she suffers for his pain.
- Miranda comes to see Ferdinand. Prospero watches the interchange unobserved.
- Miranda offers to carry the logs, but Ferdinand says he would rather break his back than allow something so dishonourable than let a woman do his work. Miranda does not understand why she cannot help.
- Miranda reveals her name and Ferdinand tells her that she is the most perfect woman that he has ever met. He states that he is only a slave because of her.
- Miranda asks if he loves her, and Ferdinand replies in hyperbolic terms. She states she will marry him if he wants her. Ferdinand kneels and agrees.
- Prospero is elated that his plan has worked to cement their love and marriage.

Questions for Act III, Scene i

1. What would be unusual about this courtship and the gender roles taken within it for the time? What does this show about Miranda and how she has been socialised by her time on the island?

Quote

> "Poor worm, thou art infected;
> This visitation shows it."
>
> (Prospero about Miranda) III, ii, 33–34

Act III, Scene ii

- Stephano, Caliban and Trinculo are seen on another part of the island, very drunk. Caliban is trying to convince the men to kill Prospero. Trinculo keeps making fun of Caliban, which upsets him.
- Ariel enters, invisible, and begins to whisper in the mens' ears, causing them to fight.
- Caliban outlines the plan, he wants them to kill Prospero during his afternoon sleep, take possession of his books and offers them Miranda's body in the future as a bribe to commit the act. They agree to the act.
- Ariel plays music. Caliban urges them to ignore it, but they follow it instead.

Question for Act III, Scene ii

1. What indicates that this is a comic act and that the audience is not supposed to take this threat seriously?

Quote

> "I say by sorcery he got this isle;
> From me he got it."
>
> (Caliban about Prospero) III, ii, 46–47

Act III, Scene iii

- The nobles are tired from wandering all over the island. They resolve to rest. Antonio and Sebastian plan to murder the King and Gonzalo as soon as they fall asleep.
- Prospero enters, but is unseen by the men. Music begins and spirits bring in a banquet, inviting the men to eat it.
- The men are amazed, but wonder if the food is safe to eat. Just as they decide to eat, the food vanishes.
- Thunder and lightning announce Ariel's entrance, who appears as a harpy.
- Ariel accuses Antonio, Alonso and Sebastian with taking Prospero out of power and throwing him and his innocent child into the sea. He states that Ferdinand has been taken because of this.
- While they are trapped in Ariel's magic, Prospero delivers a soliloquy to the audience about how his enemies are now in his power and Ferdinand is alive and loved. He leaves.
- Gonzalo has not heard the accusations. The other nobles are plagued by the guilt and dread they feel.

Question for Act III, Scene iii

1. Why does Ariel appear as a harpy? What effect does this have on the men?

Quote

> "My high charms work
> And these, mine enemies, are all knit up
> In their distractions. They are now in my power;"
> (Prospero) III, ii, 88–90

Act IV, Scene i

- Prospero has freed Ferdinand and to repay him he gives him Miranda's hand in marriage. He speaks highly of her great worth.
- Miranda listens silently as her father warns her husband to be not to take her virginity before they are married lawfully in the church, or he will curse their union. Ferdinand promises to guard her honour.
- Prospero commands Ariel to bring forth spirits to put on a show for the young couple. Ariel reminds Prospero that he has been promised his freedom before he obeys.
- Miranda and Ferdinand act as the audience, Prospero as the director and the spirits as the actors, as a theatre production is staged. The style of the production is a masque, with elaborate costumes and this style was particular to the court.
- The first spirits are dressed as Iris, the goddess of the rainbow, symbolising harmony, and Ceres, the goddess of the harvest, symbolising fertility. This shows the blessings that Prospero wishes for the young couple, and it reminds the audience that this union will bring harmony back to the provinces of Italy.
- Juno, the protector and queen comes to sing a blessing to the couple. Ferdinand realises that the actors are spirits and that Prospero commands this magic.
- They are watching a dance of spirits pretending to be nymphs and harvesters when Prospero remembers that Caliban is plotting to kill him and stops the production.
- Ferdinand is concerned, but Prospero explains in a monologue that the actors have just disappeared and just like all visions provided by theatres, vanished into nothing. He reminds him that

all men are mortal and eventually disappear anyway. He sends Ferdinand and Miranda to his cell.

- Prospero asks Ariel to fetch Caliban, Trinculo and Stephano from the dirty pond where he left them. First they lay out glittering clothes in front of the cell.
- The men enter, ready to kill Prospero in his sleep. Ariel and Prospero watch them. Caliban urges them to enter and kill Prospero quickly, but the men are distracted by the clothes. They begin to try on the garments, looking foolish in them and ignoring Caliban's pleading. They load up Caliban with all the clothes they want to take with them.
- Spirits enter in the shape of hunting dogs and chase Caliban, Trinculo and Stephano off the stage.

Questions for Act IV, Scene i

1. Why would Shakespeare include the masque in his play?
2. What does the scene with the clothes reveal about the superficial nature of Stephano and Trinculo and of their leadership ability?

Quote

"And like the baseless fabric of this vision,
The cloud-capped towers, the gorgeous palaces,
The solemn temples, the great globe itself,
Yea, all which it inherit, shall dissolve,
And like this insubstantial pageant faded
And leave not a rack behind."

(Prospero) IV, i, 151–156

Act V, Scene i

- Prospero begins the scene in his magic robes. He reiterates his promise to free Ariel soon.
- Ariel tells of the suffering that the nobles are enduring. He particularly speaks of the misery Gonzalo is displaying and states

that if he was human, he would feel sorry for them. Prospero decides that he will forgive the men and commands their release.

- In a soliloquy, Prospero details the extreme power he has wielded through his magic. He vows to give that magic up once he returns to Italy.
- The nobles enter and stand in the charmed circle Prospero has laid out on the stage. He speaks first to Gonzalo, whose charm dissolves and he can hear him speak kindly to him and thank him for saving his life. Prospero forgives Alonso, his brother and Sebastian, but reveals that he knew what Sebastian and Antonio were about to do to the King.
- Prospero changes his clothes so that the nobles will recognise him. Alonso asks his forgiveness. He embraces Gonzalo and warns Antonio and Sebastian that he won't tell their secrets at this point in time.
- Alonso reveals that he lost his son and Prospero tells him that he also lost a daughter, in the last tempest.
- Prospero opens the covering to his cell to reveal Miranda and Ferdinand playing chess. As we see them, Miranda is accusing him of cheating, then she changes her mind and tells him that he can cheat on her and she will call it "fair play".
- Ferdinand sees his father and kneels before him. Miranda is amazed by all the people as she has never seen so many men or nobles.
- Alonso accepts Miranda as his new daughter-in-law and asks her forgiveness for his part in the plan to cast her out to sea.
- The master and boatswain enter, revealing that they have all been asleep and that the boat is whole and docked in the harbour. Alonso wants to know how this has happened and Prospero promises to tell him another time.
- Ariel brings in Caliban, Trinculo and Stephano wearing the stolen clothes. Caliban knows he will be made to suffer. The men are made to get the cell ready for the nobles, reminding them of their place as servants. The nobles will stay there overnight and then sail for Italy in the morning.

- Ariel is asked to deliver strong winds to send the ship home to Naples and then he is freed.

Question for Act V, Scene i

1. Why does Prospero forgive his enemies?

Quote

"Was Milan thrust from Milan, that his issue
Should become kings of Naples?"

(Gonzalo) V, i, 205–206

Epilogue

- Prospero delivers an epilogue. He states that all he has now is his mortal power, no magic.
- In a metatheatrical address, Prospero tells the audience that they alone have the power to release him from the island and deliver him to Naples, and that they will do that with applause and cheering. He reminds the audience that he would forgive their faults, and thus they should forgive his and give him resounding applause, to free him from the confines of a despairing end.

Questions for the Epilogue

1. To what extent is this a satisfactory ending to the play?
2. Can you think of some different interpretations for the words "art" and "charm" which Shakespeare might be wanting the audience to think about in the Epilogue? Explain them.

Quote

"But release me from my bands
With the help of your good hands."

(Prospero) Epilogue 8–9

Activity

- Once you have finished the play, choose three memorable events or scenes from *The Tempest*. For each event or scene, explain how it would be viewed by Jacobeans. Now explain how each event would be perceived in a more contemporary context.

Context of *Hag-Seed*

Hag-Seed was released in 2016, to coincide with the 400 year anniversary of Shakespeare's death. The Hogarth Shakespeare Project had asked notable authors to reinterpret Shakespearean plays into prose novels and Atwood agreed to the endeavour, choosing *The Tempest* as the vehicle she wanted to reimagine. Her acceptance and choice of play is not surprising. Atwood had previously nominated Shakespeare as her favourite author and had written about Prospero and *The Tempest* before. In her book *On Writers and Writing*, she devotes a chapter to the belief that all artists are magicians and illusionists, using Prospero to illustrate her claim.

The fact that Hogarth Press, a company originally established by Virginia Woolf, would choose Margaret Atwood as one of their authors is also not surprising. Atwood is an internationally acclaimed author and poet. She has been writing since her Canadian childhood, and she decided to become a full-time writer in high school. She reached critical acclaim with her poetry, receiving the E.J. Pratt Medal for *Double Persephone* in 1961 and has gone on to win countless awards including the Booker prize, which she had won once at the time of publishing (but has won again since publishing *Hag-Seed*.) She is perhaps best known for her novels, including *Alias Grace* and *The Robber Bride*. Her speculative fiction *The Handmaid's Tale* may be her best known work, particularly as it was made into a television series and the iconic red hood of the handmaids has become a feminist symbol which is recognised globally.

While Atwood has stated that she is not a feminist writer, her strong female characters and messages often resonate with women. She addressed notions of feminism in her 1993 speech at the Cheltenham Literature Festival, arguing that characters should not be constrained by preconceived concepts of femininity. The speech has been replicated, published and is now studied as a feminist polemic.

An altruistic individual, Atwood has been known to donate her winnings from literature awards. Recipients include environmental groups and Artists against Racism, amongst others. Her postcolonial lens is evident in her novel, and she mentioned in a Guardian article that the island was stolen from Caliban by Prospero. This helps to explain the title of the novel and her focus on the plight of Caliban and the injustice towards the prisoners.

Other echoes of the context are evident in the novel. An Ontario blog called "No Books for Prisoners" had started four years earlier which had been one of the influences of the Literacy Initiative in Prisons which was running by 2016 in Canada.

Atwood's political manoeuvring echoes not just the Renaissance, but her own context as well. At the time, the Russian government was being investigated for interfering with the Trump election in the United States. Britain had also just voted to leave the EU, causing a huge split with past allies. Plus, both Brazil and South Korea had scandals breaking which turned public opinion against their presidents, and both were impeached by the end of 2016. Clearly, the deals of Tony, Sebert and Sal also relate to the modern world.

Finally, Atwood's strong female characters reflect the Canadian context as well. A country that had previously had a female Prime Minister, Canada was a setting that was far less patriarchal than Jacobean times. In 2016 the #Metoo movement had gained enormous traction with an Alyssa Milano tweet asking for solidarity and thus characterisation questioning the agency and realistic portrayal of women is relevant to the time. In what was the crest of the third wave of feminism, Anne-Marie's revision of the prisoners' fate for Miranda is a poignant reflection on changing values in society.

Questions and Activities

1. Why do you think it is relevant to consider the specific context of 2016 instead of just assuming it is your own modern context reflected in the novel?
2. Choose three scenes in the novel that reflect on what was occurring in society and explain how they help us to make connections with the contemporary audience and with the Shakespearian text.

Summary of *Hag-Seed*

Prologue: Screening

- The novel begins with a script of *The Tempest* play which the Fletcher Correctional Players will create under Felix's guidance by the end of the novel. The script form indicates that theatre is an important medium, despite the fact that *Hag-Seed* is a novel.
- Words like "flatscreen" and "camera" immediately indicate the modern context and that this is a postmodern version of Shakespeare's work.
- The dialogue mixes lines from Shakespeare with colloquial language, indicating the eclectic nature of the production.
- The props are a mixture of objects which reference the Jacobean context with strange pieces from the modern world. For example, a quill is followed by images from the "Tornado Channel". This further references the lack of funding the Correctional Players have and how they have had to be resourceful to create Shakespeare's scenes.
- At the end of the play, Ariel is shown in control of the lights and the script extends to the audience. This indicates that the politicians who have entered the prison are merely players in Felix's play and that he is directing and controlling them. Their panic foreshadows the climax of the novel.

Quotes

"Announcer: What you're gonna see is a storm at sea"

Page 3

"Closeup of Ariel in a blue bathing cap and iridescent ski goggles…Behind his left shoulder there's an odd shadow."

Page 5

Question for Prologue: Screening

- What is unexpected and unusual about this beginning for the reader? List the unexpected elements.

Part I. Dark Backward

1. Seashore

- The prose portion of the novel begins with Felix getting ready for his performance. He compares his previous life of money and celebrity to the life he is now living, which is a life of poverty in the hovel. His anger at Tony, whom he blames for his downfall, is apparent and he plans to have his revenge.
- The title, references to the hovel and Tony's political career, make it evident that this part of the narrative is set immediately before Felix airs his performance of *The Tempest*.
- Felix thinks about the art of acting and how important it is to make the audience believe in your act. He refers to it as making "magic".

Quotes

"If the words are not perfect, the pitch exact, the modulation delicately adjusted, the spell fails." Page 9

"How he has fallen. How deflated. How reduced. Cobbling together this bare existence, living in a hovel."
Felix's self-reflection, page 10

2. High Charms

- The narrative begins Felix's backstory, explaining how he came to live in the hovel.
- Twelve years ago, Felix was the Artistic Director of the Makeshiweg Festival while Tony had acted as producer and ran the administration and business elements of the festival. Felix was

content to let Tony write reports, attain the government grants and do all the administration so that Felix could work on his visions for the plays, which became more bizarre and grandiose.

- Felix's wife had died in childbirth, so he named his daughter Miranda, as he was already middle-aged, and she would be an only child. (So from birth his daughter is named after Miranda in *The Tempest*.) She only lives until the age of three, when she is killed by Meningitis. Felix refuses to believe she is lost forever.
- Felix decides to stage *The Tempest* as an homage to his daughter and so that he can resurrect her. He searches for the perfect woman to cast and finds Anne-Marie, an ex-gymnast.
- He has a cloak of plush animal skins made so he can play Prospero and becomes obsessed with his vision.

Quote

> "Right after the funeral with its pathetically small coffin he'd plunged himself into *The Tempest*. It was an evasion, he knew that about himself even then, but it was also to be a kind of reincarnation."
>
> (Felix's response to his daughter's death.) Page 15

3. Usurper

- Felix remembers the moment when Tony told him that the Board had terminated his contract as the Artistic Director of the festival. Felix knows that the Chair of the Board, Lonnie Gordon, would never have made this decision and that it must be Tony's influence.
- Tony gives him a letter of termination. He claims that Felix's version of *The Tempest* would never work as he had envisioned Caliban as a paraplegic and that and the cape would cause complaints.
- Felix threatens to go to Sal O'Nally, the heritage minister, but Tony tells him that Sal has asked Tony already to take Felix's job. Felix yells accusations at Tony.

Quote

> "The secrecy, the sabotage. The snake-like subterfuge. The stupendous betrayal. Tony had been the instigator, he'd been the implementer start to finish."
>
> (Felix reflecting on how Tony betrays him.) Page 23

4. Garment

- Tony has security escort Felix to his Mustang convertible, where his belongings wait in boxes for him. While he is packing, Lonnie turns up to apologise and states that he was outvoted on the Board and tried to keep Felix.
- Lonnie gives Felix the cloak and staff he had made for *The Tempest* and his script. Felix realises that Lonnie is crying and reflects that he was the only genuine person who also cared about Miranda.

Quote

> "Lonnie should watch his ass with Tony at the helm, thought Felix. Especially if he keeps displaying such blubbery compunction."
>
> Page 27

5. Poor Full Cell

- Felix drives aimlessly with his belongings. Eventually he sees a small two roomed shack on a low hill and investigates it. It is rustic, but has electricity and an outhouse. After finishing his current lease, he finds the owner of the shanty at the nearest farmhouse. He agrees to pay cash and tells her his name is Mr. Duke. The owner agrees not to tell anyone he is living there.

Quote

> "He would remain invisible to the world at large, for now."
>
> Page 33

6. Abysm of Time

- Felix tells people that he is a writer but finds it hard to fill his time in the hovel. He reads, gardens and tries to make the shack more habitable.
- Felix decides that he wants to stage his version of *The Tempest* somehow. He also wants revenge.

Quote

"His Miranda must be released from her glass coffin; she must be given a life."

Page 41

7. Rapt in Secret Studies

- Felix fantasises about how to best take his revenge on Tony. As he stalks him through the papers, Tony begins to get awards for programs that Felix has put into place.
- Felix sees in the news that after receiving the order of Ontario, Tony resigns as Artistic Director and runs for political office.
- Felix buys a personal computer and begins stalking both Tony and Sal online.
- Felix gradually begins to imagine that Miranda is in the hovel with him. He begins by reading aloud to her, then helps her with imaginary homework, addresses her at the dinner table and teaches her to play chess.
- Felix actually hears Miranda's voice out loud and realises how far his fantasy has grown. He decides to get a job.

Quotes

"What was Felix waiting for? He hardly knew. A chance opening, a lucky break? Page 45

"She never asked him how they came to be there together, living in the shanty, apart from everyone else."

(Felix reflecting on his imagined Miranda.) Page 47

8. Bring the Rabble

- Felix applies for a job teaching literacy through literature at the prison near him. He fakes the documents for his resume, claiming to be a retired teacher.
- Felix is interviewed for the position, but Estelle, the member of the Advisory Board, recognises him. She agrees to keep his identity a secret, offers him the job and flirts with him.
- Felix convinces Estelle to let him change the reading program to one where the prisoners are acting out Shakespeare. He promises to meet all the criteria of the literacy program as well.
- After teaching them three Shakespearean plays, Felix has had great success in the prison. He would let them use the swear words contained in the play they were studying as one tactic to engage them. The players would rewrite the parts into colloquial language and then video the scenes. The plays are then shown in the prison. Felix encourages the prisoners through a point system where they earn cigarettes which he smuggles into the cast party.
- Felix is waiting for the right time so that he can enact his plan for revenge.

Quote

> "After a stellar career like his, what a descent-doing Shakespeare in the clink with a bunch of thieves, drug dealers, embezzlers, man-slaughterers, fraudsters, and con men."
>
> Page 58

9. Pearl Eyes

- It is the fourth season of the theatre program for the Fletcher Correctional Players and Felix readies his own costume, as he wants to look like he is a non-threatening, but eccentric drama teacher.
- Miranda is fifteen in Felix's imagination at this stage, and he envisions that she is brooding about something. In his version of her she is innocent and always well behaved, unlike real teenage girls he has heard of.

- Felix glimpses Prospero's cloak at the back of his armoire and knows that it will soon be time for him to wear it.

Quotes

> "If she'd lived, she would have been at the awkward female stage: making dismissive comments, rolling her eyes at him… But none of that has happened. She remains simple. She remains innocent.
>
> (Felix considering the imaginary Miranda.) Page 62

> "He hasn't worn his mantle since that time of treachery and rupture a dozen years ago."
>
> Page 64

Questions for Part I: Dark Backward

1. What is Felix's art, or magic in this novel? What evidence is there that he is obsessed by this art?
2. The catalyst for Felix's downfall is the death of his daughter Miranda. How does the depiction of this event and his subsequent reaction to it, elicit sympathy from the reader?
3. What crimes has Tony committed, according to Felix?
4. What methods does Felix use to achieve success when working with the inmates in the prison?
5. What evidence is there that Felix has lost his grip on his sanity? What warning does this give the reader?

Part II: A Brave Kingdom

10. Auspicious star

- Estelle has told Felix a few months earlier that both Sal O'Nally and Tony Price will be visiting the prison on the day that they view the final video of this year's play. He informs her that they will perform *The Tempest* for them.

Quote

> "'The actors,' said Felix. He refused to call them troupe, he refused to call them prisoners, not while they were in his theatre troupe."
>
> Page 71

11. Meaner fellows

- The process of entering the dismal prison is described in detail. The guards are not excited about the choice of play, but Felix sells it to them by explaining that it is about revenge.

Quote

> "There will be trouble, thinks Felix, but not of the kind you mean."
>
> Page 77

12. Almost inaccessible

- As he enters the prison Felix avoids the other teachers and counsellors as they don't agree with his program and believe that Shakespeare is too violent. He does not want to explain his theory that performance is a form of "catharsis".
- Atwood describes the classrooms Felix uses to run his course as he arrives for his first day of teaching. He is locked in by the guards but insists on no cameras in the performance space.

Quote

> "This is the extent of it, Felix muses. My island domain. My place of exile. My penance. My theatre."
>
> Page 81

13. Felix addresses the Players

- Felix meets the prisoners who have signed up for his course this year. He knows many of them already and believes that the young computer hacker will be a perfect Ariel and that Antonio would best be played by the older real estate con man.
- The process of producing a play in prison is outlined. Each character has a team of understudies. They also rewrite speeches so that they work in a modern context.
- The major considerations of the play are written on the board. These are that it is a musical, that it uses magic and prisons, that it considers who is a monster and that it is focused on revenge.
- The prisoners are not excited about the choice of play until Felix tells them that he will be bringing an actress in to play Miranda.

Quote

> "Lost boys all of them, though they are not boys: their ages range from nineteen to forty-five. They are many hues, from white to black through yellow, red and brown; they are many ethnicities."
>
> (Felix reflecting on the prisoners in his course.) Page 82

14. First assignment: Curse words

- The players assemble with a list of the curse words from the play. They question why some of them are offensive and 8Handz mentions Prospero's colonial bias.

Quote

> "Prospero thinks he's so awesome and superior, he can put down what other people think."
>
> (8Handz explaining the attitude behind the insults.) Page 91

15. Oh you wonder

- Felix meets with Anne-Marie Greenland, the actress who was supposed to play Miranda in the original production of *The Tempest*. She has had a brief career as a dancer but after an injury, now choreographs.
- Felix convinces Anne-Marie to take the part. She is older and thinner, and has tattoos, but he believes she looks childlike enough for the part. He is startled by her swearing and voracious appetite. He promises to play Prospero in the production.

Quote

> "He was never ready when a slice of filth came out of her child-like mouth."
>
> (Felix about Anne-Marie) Page 97

16. Invisible to every eyeball else

- As a means of introducing her, and to warn the men of her strength, Felix shows the players a video of one of Anne-Marie's dances which is very physical.
- Nobody wants to play Ariel, so Felix leads a discussion of his qualities which brings them to the conclusion that he is a superhero or an alien. They also decide that the spirits with him are the special effects team for Prospero.

Quote

> "Now that they grasp the possibilities, they all want to be on Team Ariel."
>
> Page 105

17. The isle is full of noises

- When Felix returns to his shack he wonders if he should have left the heat on for his daughter before he reminds himself that she isn't real.
- Felix starts to consider his plan. He needs Tony and Sal to view the play in the sealed wing with him, instead of with the warden, so he can show them a separate show, which will be improvised for them.
- Felix considers giving up his plan and revenge, especially as he feels Miranda is worried. Then he sees the animal cape and is resolved.
- Felix is concerned that Miranda hasn't been given the consumables and trivialities that other teenage girls have.

Quotes

"Their hour will be his hour. His vengeful hour."
(Felix contemplating his enemies.) Page 109

"She should have what other girls her age take for granted, not that he knows what those things are."
(Felix thinking about what Miranda has missed out on in life.) Page 109

18. The island's mine

- This chapter gives a short summation of many of the characters, seen through Felix's perspective. He discusses the island and who has a right to the land. Felix goes through the different groups who claim a right to the island, starting from Sycorax, Caliban and Ariel. Their rule is overthrown by Prospero and Miranda. The nobles next arrive, and then finally the servants Trinculo and Stephano.
- Felix asks the prisoners to vote for their preferred part.

Quote

"The tempest is an illusion, but they are convinced by it: they think they've been shipwrecked."
(Explanation of how the nobles arrive on the island.) Page 114

19. Most scurvy monster

- Too many prisoners vote to play Caliban, so Felix bathes while he readies himself to talk them out of it. He must heat the water manually in the hovel and he wonders about how these things were managed by Prospero and why they are never mentioned in literature. This is metafictional, as Atwood is discussing something in literature she is saying is never discussed.
- Felix reminds the men that Caliban is not just bullied and angry, but he is also someone who has local knowledge and music, who is romantic, visionary and vengeful.
- As homework, Felix asks the men to find all the prisons that are created in the play. He states that he can see seven, though he actually knows nine.

Quote

"We get him"

(The prisoners about Caliban and why they want to play his part.) Page 120

Questions for Part II: A Brave Kingdom

1. In what way is the interpretation of *The Tempest* that Felix offers a modern interpretation?
2. What is Felix's plan for vengeance so far?
3. What are some of the methods that Felix uses to manipulate the prisoners in his course?
4. Why is it important that Anne-Marie is used to play Miranda in the production?

Part III: These Our Actors

20. Second assignment: Prisoners and Jailers

- This chapter is a collated table of the inmates' homework. They were asked to identify the prisoners and jailers in the play. The players identify only eight, but Felix has previously stated that he can perceive nine. The reader then speculates about the missing prison and jailer. (Later in the novel Felix reveals that it is the theatre and the play itself.)

21. Prospero's Goblins

- The prisoners discuss whether Prospero should have imprisoned the other characters. Felix convinces them that he has no choice but to use his magic to protect his daughter.
- The class discusses the plot to marry Miranda and Ferdinand. Whilst they disagree with the principle of arranged marriage, the players agree that it was Prospero's only chance to regain power and status.
- Felix informs them that each inmate will also have a second role as a goblin. He plans to use the goblins to menace Tony and Sal when they visit the prison.

Quote

> "He can see how it could unfold: Tony and Sal, surrounded by Goblins. Herded by them. Menaced by them."
>
> Page 131

22. The Persons of the Play

- The cast list for the play is finalised. 8Handz the young computer hacker will play Ariel. Caliban will be played by Leggs, a heavy-set war veteran with PTSD and drug issues. Ferdinand will be played by a handsome conman who looks young, called WonderBoy.

Quote

> "He'll give the men parts they have a chance of performing well: he is after all a director, first and foremost. The play's the thing."
>
> Page 133

23. Admired Miranda

- Felix meets with Anne-Marie. He brings her the cast list, which also has the convictions of each player detailed. She questions the ethics of this, but he assures her that it is so she can see that they are petty criminals and not murderers.
- Acting as a father figure, Felix warns Anne-Marie not to get conned by WonderBoy.
- Anne-Marie suggests that Disney Princess dolls are used to play the parts of the goddesses in the Masque.
- Felix suddenly wonders if Miranda wasn't innocent, but actually living in a state of fear, petrified of both her lunatic father and her potential rapist, Caliban.

Quote

> "He has a split instant of seeing Prospero through the gaze of Miranda – a petrified Miranda who's suddenly realized that her adored father is a full-blown maniac, and paranoid into the bargain."
>
> Page 143

24. To the present business

- Anne-Marie and Felix arrive at the prison. Felix quotes Richard Lovelace's poetry about the nature of imprisonment as they enter.
- Anne-Marie observes the men as they start to rehearse.
- Felix asks 8Handz to change the surveillance system so that he doesn't show up on it, in exchange for early parole.

Quote

> "You got to watch the old enchanter, he'll charm you silly."
> (Anne-Marie about Felix) Page 150

25. Evil Bro Antonio

- Felix stalks Tony and Sal's movements through the internet as he forms his plot for revenge.
- The production has five weeks to go but is experiencing problems. Wonder Boy has proposed to Anne-Marie and tried to kiss her, and she has physically restrained him, emasculating him and hampering their chemistry onstage.
- The Antonio team ask to insert a new scene into the play. Instead of Prospero telling his backstory, they want Antonio to tell the story as a flashback. Snake Eye performs the rap they have composed which reveals the story and is performed with dancers. Felix agrees to include it, and then to cut to images of the prisoners' own children who help them survive the ordeal of prison (as Miranda did for Prospero.)
- Snake Eye suggests that Felix adds his own picture of his child to the montage and Felix yells his refusal.

Quote

> "They can't possibly know anything about him, him and his remorse, his self-castigation, his endless grief."
>
> (Felix reflecting on his refusal to supply Miranda's photograph.) Page 160

26. Quaint devices

- Felix travels to Toronto for props. He visits a toy store for the boats and Disney Princess dolls. He feels he can cope with the store as Miranda is now too old for toys.
- In Toronto, Felix also picks up costumes, including goggles, bathing caps and ski masks for the goblins.

27. Ignorant of what thou art

- Felix returns from his shopping trip and shows Miranda his props. She doesn't understand them as she has no knowledge of the outside world or the theatre.
- Later, Miranda claims that she has read the play.
- The imaginary Miranda insists on playing herself in *The Tempest*. They fight about this. It is clear from this that Felix is losing his grip on reality.

Quote

> "You can't play Miranda," he says as firmly as he can. "It's not possible." This is the first time he's opposed her directly in anything. How to tell her that no one but he himself would be able to see her?"
>
> (Felix about Miranda) Page 168

28. Hag-Seed

- The cast begin rehearsing their lines and music in earnest.
- 8Handz sets up mini-cameras and speakers so that Felix can watch anything happening in the classrooms.
- Anne-Marie has adopted a matronly persona with the prisoners. She is promising to get her knitting group to make dresses for the goddesses.
- Felix spontaneously performs one of Prospero's monologues, making Anne-Marie produce both tears and profanity.
- Leggs performs a rap that tells Caliban's side of the story. They are going to perform it with back up dancers wearing lizard hats. Felix is so proud of Leggs he chokes up.

Quote

> "This place was my kingdom! And I was the king!
> I was the king of everything:
> King Hag-Seed!"
>
> (From Leggs' rap from Caliban's perspective.) Page 174

29. Approach

- Waking up and feeling hungover, Felix recognises that he has avoided facing the reality of his daughter's death.
- Stalking Tony and Sal through the internet, Felix sees that that often they have a politician with them, Sebert Stanley. He wonders how they will react when they realise that it is Felix in the prison.
- Trying on his magic cloak costume, Felix tries out some of his lines but feels they are not authentic. He panics that Prospero is too multilayered and complex a character to play.
- Miranda whispers Ariel's lines in his ear and he agrees that she can be the understudy for Ariel.

Quote

> "His voice sounds fraudulent. Where is the authentic pitch, the true note? Why did he ever think he could play the impossible part? So many contradictions to Prospero!"
>
> (Felix considering playing Prospero) Page 179

Questions for Part III: These Our Actors

1. What evidence is there that this will be an amateur production, compared to the well-funded professional productions which Felix used to direct?
2. Is Felix aware of his own mental health issues? What problems can you see that he is struggling with?
3. How are the Players gaining their own agency and starting to take control of their character's roles? Would Felix be used to this when directing past productions?

Part IV: Rough Magic

30. Some vanity of mine art

- A dream haunts Felix, and he wonders if Shakespeare was also haunted or inspired by a spirit.
- Anne-Marie is leading WonderBoy on to some extent, so that they will have chemistry onscreen.
- Felix has to talk his imaginary Miranda into riding in the car, as she is scared of it.
- When 8Handz performs his lines, he keeps hearing another voice saying them at the same time. The implication is that it is the imaginary Miranda.

Quote

> "I was hearing this weird feedback thing. Like someone was saying the lines at the same time as me."
>
> (8Handz complaining about hearing voices) Page 189

31. Bountiful Fortune, now my dear lady

- When Felix picks up the last of the costumes, he also meets a drug dealer contact of 8Handz and gets pills and a powder. The pills make people pass out for ten minutes. The powder is to provide an acid trip so he can lace the grapes.
- Estelle reveals that Tony and Sal are planning on cancelling the theatre production program. Felix is thrilled as it will give him the ammunition to incite the goblins and motivate them to attack the politicians.
- Felix learns that Sal's son Frederick is an aspiring director and that he will be coming to the jail. He has also been viewing past videos of the correctional players' work and is a fan.

Quote

> "Outrageous! A snot-nosed, silver-spooned brat who thinks he can politic his way into the theatre, fly in on Daddy's coattails."
>
> (Felix's initial impression of Freddie.) Page 196

32. Felix Addresses the Goblins

- On the day of the production, Felix injects the grapes with the drugs and smuggles them into the jail, along with the pills.
- In his preparatory speech for the actors, Felix reminds them that the politicians want to cancel the Fletcher Correctional Players.
- Some of the players are nervous about the plans they have been rehearsing, but Felix reassures them. He thanks 8Handz for putting the plan into place and organising the technical wizardry which made it possible.

Quote

> "'I couldn't have done it without Ariel," says Felix, "Without 8Handz. He's been – He's been awesome."'
>
> (Felix's speech to the players.) Page 202

33. The hour's now come

- The dignitaries arrive at the prison. Estelle is there, but not obvious. The narrative perspective switches to Sal O'Nally. He doesn't believe that prisoners can be educated.
- The politicians enter the jail. Security takes their mobile phones and gives them pagers.
- The players meet the politicians dressed as pirates. They sprinkle them with confetti and tell them that this is an interactive performance.
- While seated in the audience, Frederick meets Anne-Marie and immediately begins flirting.

Quote

> "Welcome to the good ship Tempest, which you are now aboard."
>
> (Boatswain) Page 206

34. Tempest

- This is the same chapter used to open the novel in **Prologue: Screening**. The script form is used. Readers now know why the language in the play mixes Jacobian terms and colloquial phrasing.
- In this second reading, many people would now assume that the "odd shadow" behind Ariel's shoulder refers to the imagined Miranda, who is playing the understudy for Prospero's spirit.
- Notice that the script form continues when the video stops and the politicians begin to speak, panicking that they hear gunshots. This implies that Felix is manipulating them, or directing them.

35. Rich and strange

- In the darkness the politicians are pinched and separated. They realise their pagers are gone.
- Freddie is kidnapped but the noises make it sound to the others like he is being shot.
- The line from the play, "We split" is heard when the nobles believe their ship is on fire and they have no choice but to jump in the ocean.
- Freddie finds himself isolated in an old room. He hears a song about his father being drowned. Anne-Marie comes in and tells him that the man playing Prospero is mad and that he must play the part of Ferdinand to survive. Freddie starts the lines but breaks out of his role to tell Anne-Marie that he is falling for her.

Quote

> "There's someone in here who's crazy. Crazy as a full moon dog. Thinks he's Prospero."
>
> (Anne-Marie to Freddie) Page 215

36. A maze trod

- The politicians are moved by dark figures to another room. Sal is dejected as he believes that his son, Freddie, has been shot.
- Lonnie tries to be optimistic, despite the situation. Tony and Sebert make fun of him.
- Sal and Lonnie, having been drugged, fall asleep. Tony tells Sebert that he will help him in the polls against Sal. He explains that he removed his first rival, Felix.
- Tony suggests that they kill Sal and Lonnie and blame it on rioters, then later tell the media that they were cowards. They plan to smother them with pillows. Felix is recording the conversation with his surveillance cameras.
- 8Handz uses a blast of Metallica to wake Lonnie and Sal. They catch Tony holding a pillow and he claims it is defence against bullets.

Quote

> "I kicked Felix Phillips out of my path when I was at the Makeshiweg Festival. That was the first solid rung on my ladder."
>
> (Tony to Sebert) Page 220

37. Charms crack not

- The door to the room the politicians are locked in swings open and they hear Leonard Cohen music. They are watched by Felix and 8Handz on surveillance as they walk down the hall to the grapes. A tiny speaker planted on Lonnie tells him not to eat them. The other three eat the grapes. 8Handz is jealous as he wants some of the ketamine and magic mushroom concoction they are ingesting.
- A trapdoor removes the fruit and the shadow of a huge bird is projected, dominating the room. A rap is played, telling them that this is occurring because of what they did to Felix.
- Felix checks the camera on Anne-Marie and Freddie to see that they are playing chess.

Quote

> "They've killed Freddie and it's all my fault! Because of what we did to Felix!"
>
> (Sal to the other politicians) Page 226

38. Not a frown further

- The drugged ministers all begin having a drug induced episode, whilst the sober Lonnie barricades himself behind a table.
- TimEEz and Red Coyote, dressed as Trinculo and Stephano, enter the room and start to perform. The dancers and Caliban then come in. They perform a song about the politicians being the real monsters.
- 8Handz and the imaginary Miranda both argue that the men have suffered enough and that they should be rescued.
- Felix decides that he has had enough vengeance.

Quote

> "Monster, monster, so the world's gonna know
> Just what a monster you are!
> We know what you took! White collar crook!"
>
> (Leggs as Caliban) Page 230

39. Merrily, merrily

- The politicians are returned to the original viewing room and Felix shows himself. They argue that they will have Felix arrested, but he reminds them that he has both their drug fuelled antics and disloyal conversations on video.
- Felix shows them Anne-Marie and Freddie playing chess. They quote the same lines that Miranda and Ferdinand say when Prospero reveals them playing chess in his cell. Freddie introduces Anne-Marie as his new partner.
- As Felix packs up the equipment, 8Hands tells him that he can hear lines from "Row, row, row your boat" coming through the

headphones, which is a song Felix used to sing to the infant Miranda.

- When Felix leaves, he feels disappointed, then he hears Miranda's voice reminding him of the importance of forgiveness.

Quote

> "The rarer action is/In virtue than in vengeance, he hears inside his head. It's Miranda. She's prompting him."
>
> (Felix suddenly understanding why Prospero forgives his enemies.) Page 238

Questions for Part IV: Rough Magic

1. How much of the play does Atwood actually represent in this section? Can you think of particular scenes or characters who are completely cut out?
2. How does Felix's character change in this section of the novel and what prompts that change?
3. How does Atwood try to convince the reader that the imaginary Miranda is real? Why does she do this for the reader?
4. Why does the novel repeat the chapter from the prologue? What purpose and effect does this have?

Part V: This Thing of Darkness

40. Last assignment

- Felix and Anne-Marie attend the cast party in the prison. Felix is smuggling the cigarettes in chip packets which he uses to reward the men.
- The production has been a great success and the Literacy through Literature program has been extended for five years.

Quote

> '"Let me add that this was the finest production of *The Tempest* I have ever mounted." Not for them to know it is the only one.'
>
> (Felix to the prisoners) Page 245

41. Team Ariel

- The character teams from the players give their presentations for their final assessment scores from Felix. Team Ariel have decided that Ariel isn't a fairy, that he is more a holographic projection of the weather. Felix loves this idea, very relevant in an age of climate change.

42. Team Evil Bro Antonio

- Team Antonio deliver their report about what would happen after the play. They think that because Antonio is evil, that he and Sebastian would murder everyone on the way home to gain power. In their version of the projected future, Miranda is raped and Prospero, Caliban and Miranda all end up dead.

Quote

> "The rest of them don't like this story: it's not a happy ending, and it contains no redemption."
>
> (The reaction to Team Antonio's projection) Page 253

43. Team Miranda

- Anne-Marie is offended by Team Antonio's suggestion that Miranda would be raped before they kill her. She gives a speech about the likelihood of Miranda having self-defence skills, which would have been taught to her after Caliban's failed attempted rape. She also believes that Miranda would have access to Prospero's magic.
- Anne-Marie acts out the fight scene, dancing with the dolls to show how the spirits would protect Miranda and Ferdinand.

44. Team Gonzalo

- Team Gonzalo gives their report. They remind the audience that Gonzalo is an extreme optimist. Bent Pencil also states that all the characters who have some sort of virtue in the play are also weak. However, he mentions that Gonzalo's good luck would help him to prosper. He believes that Gonzalo will set up his own republic to test his theories.

45. Team Hag-Seed

- Caliban's team present his fate. They think that if he was left behind on the island he would be king of nothing. They think that a second option would be that he would be taken to Europe and exhibited as a curiosity.
- Their favoured option is the theory that Prospero secretly knew Sycorax earlier and fathered Caliban. He would then acknowledge him and teach him to be gentle. He would later become a famous musician.

Quote

> "Caliban is like his bad other self. Like father, like son."
>
> (Team Caliban on their theory) Page 267

46. Our revels

- The cast begin to celebrate. Leggs has written a musical number about Caliban's life after *The Tempest*. The theme is freedom from imprisonment. The men want to write a whole play about Caliban's fate.

Quote

> "Felix is intrigued: Caliban has escaped the play. He has escaped from Prospero like a shadow detaching itself from its body and skulking off on its own."
>
> Page 272

47. Now are ended

- The players ask about the ninth prison. Felix explains that at the end Prospero asks the audience for their indulgence and forgiveness. He asks them for applause to set him free from the island.
- As Felix leaves the prison, he feels that Miranda is with him and is sad to be losing her new friends.

Quote

> "Prospero is a prisoner inside the play he himself has composed."
>
> (Felix to the prisoners) Page 275

Questions for Part V: This Thing of Darkness

1. Why do the prisoners get so depressed about Caliban's fate when discussing their projections? What connects the men to Caliban?
2. Why can't Anne-Marie accept Miranda's powerlessness and lack of agency in the future projections?
3. In all the future fates offered by the teams, which ones are the most contextually realistic, from your knowledge of Shakespeare's world?

Epilogue: Set Me Free

- After the party, Felix packs up his shanty. His landlords have deserted the farm and turned off his electricity.
- Felix has his old job back as Artistic Director, but he plans to work behind the scenes. He has hired Freddie to direct and Anne-Marie as the choreographer, and he enjoys watching them together.
- Felix is about to go on a cruise and he plans to take 8Handz with him. He has arranged 8Handz' parole so that he can help him give lectures on the Fletcher Correctional Players whilst on the boat.
- In an epiphany, Felix realises that he needed the play to help him to let go of Miranda. He says the lines Prospero said to free Ariel and farewells her spirit.

Questions for Epilogue: Set Me Free

1. Do you believe that Felix is offered a more positive future than that given to Prospero? Argue why or why not, based on their characterisation and the endings of each text.
2. What was innovative about the structure and style that Atwood used? Discuss some of the structural and stylistic aspects you did not expect from the novel and explain what made them effective or distracting.

Themes or Issues of the Texts in Conversation

The themes in the texts are:

- Power
- Imprisonment
- The Treatment of Women
- Relationships and Making Connections
- Vengeance and Forgiveness
- Magic and Theatre
- Chaos, Status and the Other

Power

Power is a theme which is integral to both *The Tempest* and *Hag-Seed*. As the usurped Duke of Milan, it is Prospero's fall from power which motivates his plan for vengeance. To gain power, Antonio has agreed to give Naples ultimate power over Milan. Thus, by marrying Miranda to Ferdinand, Prospero is attempting to realign the power imbalance in the Italian provinces. This political power shifting all occurs, not in Italy, but on the island. The twelve years that Prospero has waited and the fortuitous circumstance of Alonso's boat sailing within reach of Prospero all allow for a dynamic shift in power to occur by the end of the play.

This political manoeuvring is echoed in Hag-Seed through the political careers of Tony and Sal. After removing Felix from his role in the Makeshiweg Festival, Tony rises up the political ranks, eventually coming into Felix's grasp as he oversees the theatre program for the Fletcher Correctional players and plans a publicity visit. Due to globalisation and international travel in the modern world, no-one is ever separated completely by physical distance in the first world, so Atwood replicates the distance between the nobles and Prospero by using Felix's hovel and the divide between the backwoods country towns and the culturally elite city and their inner social circles. Felix bridges the gap only via the internet, this magic showcasing the shifting ministerial duties of Tony and Sal for the reader.

Shakespeare not only displayed power through political means, but reflected King James' preoccupation with witch hunts and the supernatural in his gifted protagonist. Prospero has studied the dark arts extensively and Gonzalo has smuggled his magic books aboard Prospero's vessel when he escapes. This power allows him to free Ariel from the cloven pine that Sycorax has imprisoned him in, establishing Prospero's power over the airy spirit as his liberator. Prospero's power is symbolised by the titular tempest itself which establishes the plot. Both Miranda and Ariel make it clear to the audience that it is Prospero's power over nature which has created the storm. Shakespeare makes Prospero's power evident onstage by often placing him onstage watching his machinations unfold. Ariel's presence onstage, often unseen by the actors, is a further representation that Prospero is watching and manipulating the action.

Atwood reinvents Prospero's power in various ways. Devoid of an audience who believe in supernatural magic, Atwood instead pays homage to Shakespeare himself in Felix's characterisation. Felix's talent is for directing Shakespearian plays which shock and inspire audiences, a talent which has led to his usurping, yet allows him to gain favour with Estelle and the Fletcher Correctional Players. When Felix is hired by Estelle, it is his reputation which precedes him and secures his employment. When Felix adopts the pseudonym of Mr Duke for the prison, this is a reminder that he has raised his status by accepting this position as teacher.

Felix also asserts his power through blackmail and coercion. His plan involves drugging former enemies, taping their antics and then using the tapes to force them to accept his terms. This abuse of power is illegal and unethical. Atwood is reminding the reader how using tricks and arts to manipulate and coerce may not be moral or ethical and that vengeance can lead to a misuse of power.

Felix replicates Prospero's presence onstage through the surveillance cameras which 8Handz installs so that they can view the politicians. However, not all of Prospero's abuses of power were replicated.

One dynamic which Atwood does not wholly reflect is the power imbalance between Prospero and Caliban. A reflection of colonial attitudes to Caliban's

Algerian heritage, and the Shakespearean Eurocentric beliefs, Prospero's abuse of the island's original inhabitant is shocking to a modern audience. Prospero displays a clear lack of empathy for the character whom he has cast as his slave, submitting him to physical and psychological torture. The modern audience's disgust and disbelief in Caliban's treatment is evident in the fact that Atwood named her novel after the character's derogatory name, yet cast no single character to represent him. The representation of the prisoners as Caliban figures, and their consistent desire to give Caliban a voice, finally reflected in his rap and his revisionist ending, reveals a desire to give the man the power and agency denied to him by the Italian nobles.

Quote

> "I have bedimmed/
> The noontide sun, called forth the mutinous winds."
> (Prospero using personification of the elements to emphasise his power.) V, i, 41–42

Imprisonment

As Felix points out to the prisoners, there are nine different forms of prisons in *The Tempest*. Atwood is showcasing to readers that there is a recurrent theme of imprisonment which is embedded in the Shakespearean text.

The island itself is a prison, as it forms part of Prospero's punishment for ignoring his duties as a Duke and immersing himself in black magic. The penal aspect of this setting is reinforced by Atwood when she chooses the prison as Felix's secondary setting for his isolation. Atwood is reminding readers of the extreme limitations and restrictions of literal prisons by including scenes with the guards and showing Felix being subject to security screenings. Yet Felix is able to circumvent the rules of the prison, smuggling drugs and cigarettes into the facility. Just like Prospero, the prison he ends up in is not a particular challenge to the protagonist. This is a reminder that despite Alonso and Antonio's attempt to exile and assassinate Prospero, his eventual destination of the island does not become a punitive punishment. His imprisonment does not prevent him from practising his magic. The usual rules of nature do not apply to the protagonist.

Ariel's imprisonment in a cloven pine and Prospero's subsequent ability to free the spirit with his magic has created the servant and master dynamic which exists between these two characters. Ariel moves from his wooden prison to servitude, and from his many pleas for freedom, it is evident that he desires to be released from Prospero's control. This is replicated to an extent by Atwood in 8Handz, the computer hacker who performs Felix's technical magic for him, but is pent in the prison. For his services, Felix arranges an early release for 8Handz as one of the conditions when blackmailing the ministers. Just like Ariel, 8Handz is freed for his services to Felix.

Atwood alludes to the imprisonment of women within the patriarchal system through her depiction of Felix's Miranda. A creature of Felix's imagination, the Miranda of the novel is largely confined to the hovel and is defined by the habits and characteristics that Felix can imagine women having today. This echoes the way that Prospero controls his own daughter, socialising her to accept the paradigms of the Italian nobles despite their island environment. Her restricted upbringing is mitigated to some extent by their restricted environment and Prospero's frustration. He educates her beyond that which Miranda would have received in Italian society.

The final prison that Felix identifies in the play is the prison of the play itself. Discussed in the epilogue, Prospero appeals to the audience to set him free from the island and let him leave by applauding his performance. Blurring the boundaries between actor, director and character, the epilogue breaks the fourth wall as it asks the audience to allow Prospero to leave the island, giving them the power to forgive him. However, by writing *Hag-Seed*, Atwood has liberated Prospero from the island. The novel breaks the cycle of Prospero having to endlessly perform his character's duties on the island and beg for forgiveness each night. Instead, the protagonist has been liberated from both the space and era that imprisoned him. In her epilogue, Atwood gives the protagonist a future that is across oceans and far from his prison.

Quote

> "Let your indulgence set me free."
>
> *The Tempest* Epilogue, line 20

The Treatment of Women

The Tempest only has one female character who appears onstage, Prospero's daughter, Miranda. She first appears to speak freely onstage, boldly accusing her father of errant behaviour as he has created a tempest with his powers. However, the fact that she has been raised to comply with Italian noble standards is evident almost immediately to the audience. Prospero has kept important information from her and his patriarchal rule over his daughter is obvious. This is established symbolically for the audience when Prospero uses his magical powers to force her to sleep so he can instruct Ariel without her knowledge.

A further reminder of the patriarchal dominance over Miranda and the establishment of Italian Catholic values is the constant reaffirmation of Miranda's virginity. As Ferdinand falls in love with Miranda, he constantly checks whether she is a suitable bride for a prince by asking for reassurances that she is pure. Prospero also guards her chastity fiercely, reminding Ferdinand of its value. Miranda has absorbed this value system, her hatred of Caliban stemming from his attempt to steal her virginity.

While Miranda has adopted this value system, she is not wholly civilised, she is the person who proposes to Ferdinand, which would have shocked the Jacobean audience. Once she is surrounded by Italian men and accepted by society, she loses this agency and is nearly always silent or speaks in a submissive manner. Her diminished role is echoed by the diminished role of women in the play, Claribel and Sycorax, who once they are married or mothers are silenced and irrelevant and thus do not appear onstage. This is symbolic of the role of women in Jacobean England.

Atwood brings women to the forefront by increasing the amount of female characters in her novel. She introduces Estelle, the spirit or guiding star who has brought Felix to the prison. As a modern woman in business, Estelle has agency and power. It is through Estelle that Felix is able to achieve his plan. Felix listens to her and must negotiate with Estelle to get what he wants, a clear shifting of power in this society.

Atwood also splits the character of Miranda into two different personas, imagined Miranda and Anne-Marie.

The imagined Miranda is a result of Felix's grief as his daughter has perished due to meningitis at three years of age. Felix begins borrowing library books for the daughter he should have had and then begins to hear and see his imagined Miranda. This daughter takes the form of Felix's version of an ideal woman. After arguing (essentially with himself) that his depiction of her is too stereotypical, Miranda adds Maths to her repertoire of cooking and singing and begins to learn chess. By making Miranda a hallucination, with little agency, Atwood is indicating that this ideal woman only exists now in the minds of men.

As a character foil to Miranda, Atwood provides the very real Anne-Marie so that readers can view the representation of an actual woman in this contemporary era. Anne-Marie has had a failed career as a dancer, but despite this injury she is still muscular and athletic enough to fight grown men. She drinks beer, eats steak and has tattoos which remind her of former lovers. Felix's reactions to these elements show that they are unexpected character traits for him. Yet the relationship he develops with Anne-Marie is reminiscent of a paternal one. She swears at him and whilst he doesn't like the language, he accepts the rebukes. She becomes one of the few people whom Felix listens to properly. Atwood is reminding readers that the patriarchal system is outdated and that relationships now work on different levels.

Quote

> "She ought to choose a safer career path, such as medicine, or perhaps dentistry. And marry a stable and loving husband eventually of course."
>
> (Felix discussing his wishes for Miranda's future.) Pages 167–8

Relationships and Making Connections

The Tempest emphasises the importance of human connections and relationships. Isolated with his only daughter, Prospero struggles to connect to the entities on the island due to his value system and beliefs. His belief in his own superiority prevents him from connecting to Caliban, having cast him out as he threatens Miranda. Ironically, this threat stems from Caliban's own desire to form a relationship and his frustration at being relegated to a lower stratification below Prospero and his daughter, despite his prior occupation of the isle.

Prospero's desire for connection has led him to educate his daughter as his companion and her ability to play chess and match wits with Ferdinand reveals Prospero's success in this endeavour. Yet the protagonist does not view his daughter as an equal, manipulating her and controlling her emotionally and physically. This control is echoed by Atwood in her manifestation of Miranda, who is merely a product of Prospero's mind and thus at the mercy of his imagination.

Felix desires more connection and human interaction than he receives in his provincial Canadian hovel. He recognises that his interactions with his visions of Miranda are not healthy, and this instigates his search for employment and his role teaching the Fletcher Correctional Players. Atwood is reminding readers here that Shakespeare's protagonist probably felt isolated despite the company of his daughter as he did not believe her a worthy companion.

Felix develops a strong bond with the prisoners, something which is vastly different to the play. He has taken them through three Shakespearean plays before they attempt *The Tempest* and has developed a rapport with many of the men. He understands how to manage and manipulate them to achieve his goals and they have a healthy respect for their teacher and director. This is interesting as the men to a large extent symbolise Caliban and they often exhibit their connection with the Algerian servant. Atwood is commenting on the fact that in this postcolonial world, many of the racial and prejudicial divides based on colonial beliefs have been left in the past. Yet besides 8Handz, Felix does not liberate the rest of the prisoners and leaves them behind in the prison, just as Prospero would have left Caliban.

The bond Felix has with 8Handz mirrors that of Prospero and Ariel. Without peers of his own rank or status, the protagonists of both texts form bonds with their right-hand men, or spirit in Ariel's case. With Ariel, Prospero reveals his inability to form a healthy relationship, constantly threatening him or promising rewards to the spirit to manipulate him. With 8Handz, Felix learns to listen in a more mature manner. With both 8Handz and Anne-Marie, Felix exhibits a developing humility. He allows them to suggest directorial changes and accepts their advice about the play and the plan.

Atwood's protagonist is a far more rounded character than Prospero. Atwood's use of free indirect discourse also helps to showcase Felix's inner thoughts to the audience, establishing connections and relationships which are deeper and more nuanced than those attributed to Prospero. However, it is worth remembering that Shakespeare was limited by his form and that soliloquies and staging often don't allow the scope of a prose protagonist.

Quote

> "His lost Miranda, three years old, on her swing, up in the sky, in her silver frame. *That did preserve me.*"
>
> (Felix, distraught after the prisoners want to put pictures of their family in the show to demonstrate their connections that help them survive the prison.) page 160

Vengeance and Forgiveness

A major theme in both *The Tempest* and the reimagined work is vengeance. Prospero establishes for the audience that the reason for the titular tempest is his knowledge that the Italian nobles who wronged him have sailed too close to the isle. His revelation to Miranda that he was once nobility and that he was usurped by his brother Antonio establishes his desire for vengeance. It is Prospero's need for revenge that drives the plot and motivates him throughout the play. The presence of Ariel, who tortures, separates and disorients the nobles, is a reminder of Prospero's vitriol towards those who have cast him out of Italy.

Antonio feels little remorse for his actions, in fact he urges Sebastian to usurp his own brother, encouraging him to commit murder to gain power. This scene condemns Antonio in the audience's eyes and makes Prospero's desire to avenge his past appear more moral.

Shakespeare ultimately promotes forgiveness over revenge, despite the ill fortune suffered by Prospero and Miranda. When Ariel campaigns for empathy for the nobles, Prospero easily acquiesces, admitting that the "rarer action is/ In virtue than in vengeance". He aligns himself with the values of compassion and empathy, emotions which Miranda has been continuously exhibiting throughout the play. When Atwood mirrors this, she reveals that empathy was a facet of Felix's character, albeit one he had lost touch with. As the imaginary Miranda displays compassion, we are reminded that as a product of Felix's mind, this is merely a display of his own beliefs and values, manifested in a manner that the protagonist can use to meter his own conflicting emotions.

Prospero appears to forgive his brother, choosing to not tell Alonso of the murderous plot that would easily have his brother arrested and likely executed, Felix however, does not quite completely conquer his duelling emotions. He blackmails Tony and Sal with footage of their drug fuelled antics and the encounter where he reveals he has set them up is hostile and lacks the benevolence exhibited in this scene of the play. It is only in retrospect that Felix is able to harness his emotional baggage and begin to heal.

Quote

> "Twenty consciences
> That stand 'twixt me and Milan, candied be they
> And melt."
> (Antonio on how he does not feel any guilt.) II, i, 281–3

Magic and Theatre

The protagonists of each text possess a talent that makes them powerful and unique. For Prospero, it is his ability to use magic and harness the supernatural. The titular tempest itself is a reminder of his powers and the fact that Prospero is in control of the island and the spirits within it. He displays an ability to render pine and free Ariel, to stop the weapons of Ferdinand and the nobles and to inflict pain and torture on men. This art has been learned from his magic book and staff, which Gonzalo hid on the boat for him. The Jacobean audience, for whom King James was a major influence, would believe that this power was evil and should not be trusted, particularly due to James' interest in hunting witches. The exhibition of magic, as Ariel taunts the nobles when invisible, or appears as a harpy, would be shocking and titillating to the audience.

To replicate this in the modern world, Atwood casts theatre and directing itself as Felix's art. His talent is his ability to convince actors to follow him into completing his vision, just as Anne-Marie does when she agrees to play Miranda in the prison. Or 8Handz when he agrees to play Ariel, a character that the inmates believe is essentially a fairy. But just as the audience would react in Shakespeare's time, so would Atwood's readers. Essentially, the audience for the novel are readers who know and love Shakespeare, so the outrageous versions he directs, such as including spaceships in Pericles or using barbie dolls to play the goddesses in the masque, would be humorous to them.

To show that Felix has some modern magic, technology is used. The internet, computers and cameras help Felix to have control. Yet it is the fur cloak which Artwork utilises as a symbol of the protagonist's art and desire to use his directing which functions as a testament to Felix's ability to control his fate and determine his outcome. Just like Prospero, when Felix is finished with the cloak, he is finished with his art. He gives up directing and moves to a simpler existence, allowing control to pass to the next generation.

Quote

> "Wow them with wonder, as he says to his actors, *Let's make magic.*"
>
> (Felix preparing to perform the play.) page 10

Chaos, Status and the Other

The original play is essentially about reasserting the original values of the time. It is a play that begins in chaos. The mariners are frantically fighting a storm and desperately trying to stay afloat and begin barking orders at the nobles. The King and the nobles are shocked by their treatment and Gonzalo believes that he will live to hang the boatswain who has spoken to them so rudely. This is a display of chaos; the serving class are being given status whilst the ruling class are given orders.

The chaos has been orchestrated by a usurped Duke. His intervention further leads to Prince Ferdinand being captured and the King becoming destitute. The insinuation is that by interrupting the Divine Chain of Being, the nobles have led to their own downfall and caused chaos in the stratification. This is further evident when the audience sees Trinculo and Stephano onstage, appearing to try to take power. The fact that the butler is drunk instead of serving drinks is a reminder that the correct order has been disrupted. The insinuation that Trinculo and Stephano would be fit to rule is ridiculed when they put on the noble garments and look foolish, as they are not meant to wear these clothes. However, when Prospero dons his Duke's attire, Caliban can easily see that he is of higher standing than the men he has chosen to follow.

Prospero's ability to create chaos and intention to restore order is evident in the chaos of the antimasque and the symbolic images of harmony represented in the masque. He is creating a union to ensure the future of Milan and Naples, and this requires stability. By showcasing the young couple playing chess, Prospero is indicating that his daughter is the correct status to take the rank of Princess and that she has been educated in courtly ways. When Atwood replicates this scene, it is less about revealing Anne-Marie's suitability to the audience and more a courting ritual. Yet it does become a scene of order and harmony whilst the politicians are engaged in a psychotropic rampage.

Hag-Seed's representation of Jacobean social stratification indicates that transitioning from one status level to another is easier in modern times. Felix drops quickly to a level of poverty without a job and can no longer afford health care. Tony moves quickly through the ranks from theatre director to the Minister of Heritage. She also shows women in positions of high status, like Estelle, and some, like Anne-Marie, who can only escape the cycle of relative poverty with assistance.

In both texts, one group sits outside this class system. They are recognised as not belonging and thus not worthy to have a place in the social stratification. Being the son of the Algerian witch Sycorax and thus not Italian, Caliban is not seen as part of the social system. He is seen as a slave, not a servant and this is explained to the audience as due to the fact that he has threatened Miranda's virginity. His otherness is mainly due to the colonial attitudes of the nobles and this would be reflected in the prejudice of the original audience. Despite Caliban's inhabitance of the island before Prospero and his benevolence to him, he is treated poorly and his attempts to gain control of the island are ridiculed and result in punishment. The message is that those that do not belong to the stratification system cannot enter it and have no place in this society. This is evidenced by the fact that the nobles appear to intend to leave him on the island when they depart for Italy.

Atwood continuously points out this prejudice in her novel. The prisoners clamouring to play Caliban are a reminder that his fate resonates with them. They too, have been cast out from society and they will have little opportunity to successfully move through the social levels once they leave the prison system. When given an opportunity to envision the ending for the characters, nearly all the prisoners imagine that Caliban leaves the island with the Italians. In the most popular of the suggested endings, Team Hag-Seed suggests that Caliban is revealed to be Prospero's son and then becomes a famous musician. In this imagined version, Caliban is given the ultimate status of both the Jacobean audience and the modern era, elevating him to the upper echelons of society.

Quote

> "'Why is earth such an insult?' say Leggs… 'Colonialism' says 8Handz."
>
> (The prisoners discussing Caliban's insults.) page 91

Characters in the Texts

As this is a unit on Textual Conversations, each character will be discussed in *The Tempest*, and then in *Hag-Seed*. The characters in the original text are reframed and to an extent reimagined in the novel, and thus are a means of conversation between the texts.

The **Textual Conversation** section at the end of each character explanation considers how the character portrayals by Shakespeare and Atwood align or collide and whether the later text is influenced by Shakespeare in Atwood's reimagining.

Prospero in *The Tempest*

Prospero is the usurped Duke of Milan who has been stranded on the island for twelve years when the play begins. His brother decided to take his Dukedom due to Prospero's immersion in his study of the dark arts, and his knowledge of magic has helped him to gain control over the island, allowing him to free Ariel and to enslave Caliban. His ability to wield magic and create the titular "Tempest" is the first thing the audience learns about him, so they immediately recognise that he is a magician of great power and accomplishment. Jacobean audiences would be both scandalised and thrilled by these ideas, as it would be against their religious values. When he later vows to give up magic and choose a mortal and virtuous path, they would believe that he was redeeming himself.

While Prospero does not have the guns or firepower that traditional Imperial invaders had, his magic becomes a symbol of power and cultural dominance over the island. Shakespeare uses the setting and Prospero's characterisation to represent Imperialism and how the Europeans were expanding their territories and treating native people. Despite the chance to start anew and establish any type of colony (an opportunity pointed out by Gonzalo) Prospero takes control of the island and quickly establishes the cultural and social paradigms of his own lands. Miranda is silenced and controlled by him, reminding us of patriarchal rule and Caliban's treatment shows his prejudicial and imperial beliefs.

A defining aspect in Prospero's character is his desire for revenge. The plot that is unfolding is complex as he has developed a complicated plan for his revenge. He primarily focuses on making Alonso pay for his sins through his mistaken grief but does save the King from death at the hands of his brother, though only to save Gonzalo from the same fate. He later warns Sebastian and Antonio that he may uncover their secrets, but keeps their reputations safe for a time. Whilst he protects the secrets of the nobles who have wronged him, he parades the sins of Trinculo, Stephano and Caliban, bringing them into a public space, still drunk on their masters' alcohol and wearing their clothes. Clearly, he believes that the lower classes do not deserve the same forgiveness as the nobles.

Prospero as a character breaks the fourth wall, particularly in the epilogue. He has laid the groundwork for this earlier, as the play within the play has established Prospero as the director. In his final words, Prospero asks for forgiveness for any faults that we have seen, allowing for the theory that this may be Shakespeare speaking through Prospero, as the director, asking for us to appreciate his work and not to condemn it. He then begs the audience for applause so that he can return to Naples, requiring a suspension of disbelief that the character is real and can be released from the play. This metatheatrical ending changes the meaning of Prospero's magic, as it could now mean that his magic is the theatre, or it could be referring to his supernatural powers from the play. Either way, when the audience applaud, they feel that they are enabling Prospero to escape the confines of his island.

Quote

> "Now my charms are all o'erthrown
> And what strength I have is mine own
> Which is most faint."
>
> (Prospero) Epilogue 1–3

Felix in *Hag-Seed*

Atwood's protagonist is Felix Phillips, a fired theatre director from a Canadian theatre festival company. Whilst Felix never has the kind of power that Prospero wields, Atwood structures the novel so that the prologue features a scene which foreshadows the power that Felix will have once he uses the prisoners, technology and opportunity to his advantage. In everyday life though, Felix is limited in power. His strengths lie in his ability to manipulate people like Estelle and 8Handz to help him, and in his passion for the theatre, which is infectious.

Felix's passion for the theatre is all consuming. It is what has kept him away from his family so that he has missed his own daughter's death. His visions for the Shakespearean productions are so farfetched that they become parody, including elements like vampires and spaceships. It is his obsession that allows Tony to turn the Board of Directors against Felix and fire him. But his knowledge of Shakespeare is also how he connects to the prisoners, cleverly staging violent plays like Julius Caesar and Macbeth so the men can get used to the productions and will trust him. His understanding of *The Tempest* and his intelligence is continually displayed whenever he is faced with a challenge, for example when no man wanted to play Ariel. His ability to convince them that Ariel was an alien and special effects expert persuades twelve prisoners to apply for Ariel's part in the play.

The plot that Felix puts into place to make his enemies suffer is quite cruel. They would believe they were helpless in a prison riot and that people were being shot. His use of psychotropic drugs and sleeping potions also indicates that he has little regard for the law or what is morally right, also displayed when he is smuggling in cigarettes or spying on the politicians. His revenge is evidence of his anger towards Tony and Sal and how patiently he has been waiting to make them suffer.

Felix's humanity is evident in the novel, primarily through his interactions with the prisoners and Anne-Marie. He allows them to change his precious script, gives them licence to make up scenes and listens to their theories about the characters. With both 8Handz and Anne-Marie he takes a fatherly role, getting parole for 8Handz and being very protective over Anne-Marie. His later decision to leave the Makeshiweg festival in her and Freddie's capable hands shows his growing trust in her.

One troubling aspect in Felix's character is his consistent imagining of his dead daughter Miranda. After her death at the age of three and his later self-isolation, Felix starts reading books out loud to Miranda and then begins to imagine they are having meals together and living in the shack. He hears her singing and has long conversations with her. These delusions persist until he stages *The Tempest*, where he imagines she is travelling to the prison. When he can look at her picture and release her from his deluded imaginings, Felix is able to accept that his daughter is gone.

Quote

> "'It's not my play,' says Felix. 'It's our play.' Does he believe this?
> Yes. No. Not really.
> Yes."
>
> Page 176

Textual Conversations about Prospero and Felix

The main characters of each text are similar, as essentially Atwood has reimagined Prospero in a contemporary context. To make it fit Atwood's postmodern text, the second meaning of Prospero's "art to enchant" from the epilogue, his ability to direct or create theatre, has become Felix's defining feature. But both characters have a similar role, they seek revenge for injustice they perceive done to them for the usurping of their roles and they eventually forgive their enemies.

The mental health of Atwood's protagonist is questioned, due to his response to grief and his subsequent seclusion. This makes the reader question what effect seclusion on the island may have had on Prospero, and helps to view him in a favourable light.

Both characters have strong patriarchal values, though Felix eventually learns to rely on Estelle and Anne-Marie. Prospero's social paradigms remain unchallenged as he returns to a position of relative power, whilst Felix shows he is equal to 8Handz when he takes him on the cruise with him.

Ariel in *The Tempest*

Ariel in the play is the spirit whom Prospero has freed from a cloven pine and who now serves him. Imprisoned by the witch Sycorax as he refused to perform what she ordered, Ariel often seems almost human, providing his magical masters with a moral compass. It is his suggestion that Prospero forgives his enemies which is the catalyst for his master's epiphany.

Ariel creates the tempest with his powers in the beginning of the play. He is able to appear as fires on the ship, making the nobles desert the ship. He has the power to make the ship's crew sleep and to control the spirits who perform the masque. His power is substantial, and it is obvious why Prospero is so reluctant to part with him.

Ariel has served Prospero faithfully and repeatedly requests his freedom throughout the course of the play. His anger and frustration occasionally surface, but he controls it because he believes Prospero's threat that he will leave him trapped in a cloven tree again. He also trusts Prospero to honour his agreement to free him. Ariel is often placed onstage with Caliban and their different attitude to their master is juxtaposed, revealing that Ariel is accepting and optimistic about his servitude. Yet it is important to remember that in this comparison Ariel has more relative freedom and more reason to hope that he will soon be released from the situation.

8Handz in *Hag Seed*

In the novel, Ariel's counterpart is largely 8Handz, a very young computer hacker of East Indian origin who has convictions for crimes such as forgery, identity theft and impersonation. These crimes all indicate a character who deals in deception and tricking the public. However, like Ariel, 8Handz does have a moral compass as the character list that Felix gives Anne-Marie states that he believed that he was acting against the capitalists and he was a "benevolent Robin Hood".

8Handz is Felix's technological support in the prison. He wires up the secret cameras and helps to create separate tapes of *The Tempest* so that the people outside his rooms don't know what he is doing to the politicians. He also gives him the contact for the drug dealer who supplies him with the sleeping drug and the psychotropic drug he laces the grapes with during the event. He keeps Felix's secrets and is later rewarded for this, as Felix organises an early parole from the prison in return for his presence on the cruise discussing the Fletcher Correctional Players.

While 8Handz is performing Ariel, he begins to hear a second voice echoing his lines. This indicates that to an extent the imaginary Miranda is Ariel as well.

Textual Conversations about Ariel

Atwood reimagines Ariel in this contemporary world as a technological genius who is able to help the older Felix achieve his plan. While the Fletcher Correctional Players reference aliens and show clips of the weather channel to indicate Ariel's power, the characterisation of 8Handz reminds readers that the essence of Ariel is about magic, which works with our current suspension of disbelief. The contemporary audience will not believe that an elemental spirit creates tempests, but they can believe that incriminating evidence can be gained through surveillance and that tiny microphones can project a voice. When 8Handz begins to question whether he hears Miranda's voice over his headphones, it does make the reader begin to question whether the spirit Felix has imagined has taken form and why Atwood would suggest this. This feature makes the narrator unreliable to us and makes us question the nature of the reality represented to us, just as the spirits on the island would for the believing Jacobeans.

Miranda and women in *The Tempest*

Miranda is the only woman who appears onstage in the play, and she is a pivotal character. As Prospero's daughter, she has been one of only two human contacts he has had for twelve years and as a result, he has educated her more thoroughly than noble women would have been educated at the time. Her ability to match wits with Ferdinand is evident when she plays the noble game of chess, but her understanding of a woman and wife's role is evident when she claims that he can cheat at the game, and she will defend it as honourable.

Miranda has taken on her father's views in many aspects. Her disgust when she talks to Caliban is evidence that she has adopted his Imperial attitudes. It could also be argued that as she has lived a protected existence, the only bad experience that has befallen her is the attempted rape by Caliban, thus she is proof that innocence remains until experience changes those innocent beliefs.

Miranda has lived on the island for twelve of her fifteen years and thus she has had limited experiences. She is amazed by the array of men when she finally meets the nobles. Her lack of understanding of courtship rituals is evident when she asks Ferdinand if he loves her, and then later if he wants to marry her. However, she does know that she holds the prized possession for women of Western civilisation, that of virginity, plus she understands that she is noble, so she knows she is a match for the prince. Her further knowledge of Western society is obvious when Miranda stops speaking. When her father and her future husband are together and have arranged her marriage, Miranda barely speaks, revealing her lack of agency and power. When the nobles congregate, she again says few lines, revealing that she understands that she is not in a position of power.

Miranda has many of the stereotypical aspects of a woman. She is overly emotional in the first scenes and despairs for the sailors caught in the tempest. Prospero's tolerance of these hysterics seems short, and he continually puts her to sleep, representing his power over her as the patriarch.

The second daughter mentioned is Claribel, Alonso's daughter who has been married to the King of Tunisia. References to Claribel remind the audience of the ownership that men have over women and the fact that these men have delivered Claribel, like a package, and are now returning, is a reminder of how little agency women had over their own destiny.

The third woman discussed is Sycorax, the witch who was Caliban's mother. The revelations that she has treated Ariel badly and wanted him to do despicable things with his magic make her the antithesis of Miranda, a woman with no power and a sympathetic nature. The audience are supposed to recognise Miranda as an ideal woman, who will partner Ferdinand and ensure that Prospero's grandchildren rule Naples and Milan.

Quote

> "Nor have I seen
> More that I may call men than you, good friend,
> And my dear father."
>
> (Miranda to Ferdinand) III, i, 51–52

Anne-Marie, Miranda and women in *Hag-Seed*

Anne-Marie Greenland was the actress that Felix had hired to play his Miranda for his original production. When he mounts the production, twelve years later, he finds that due to a dancing injury her career has stalled, and she is willing to accept a contract to work in the prison. While she appears to be able to project the vulnerability required to play Miranda, Anne-Marie is not particularly innocent or vulnerable. She eats burgers, drinks beer and has a tattoo which she later reveals was a legacy of an affair with the actor playing Ariel. Her swearing often shocks Felix, who tends to take a paternal role with her. Her dance videos are extremely physical and show her power, which Felix uses to warn the men of her strength to protect her in the prison. While in the prison, she becomes maternal, looking after the men and knitting costumes for the dolls.

Anne-Marie becomes attached to the character of Miranda as she plays the role, but she is not able to understand the lack of agency she would have as a Jacobean woman. When the prisoners put forward the argument that Miranda would most likely be raped after the villains took control on the way home from Naples, she is unable to accept this fate. Her argument that Miranda would have magic and could fight is preposterous and reveals her inability to understand the complete lack of power and agency that Miranda would have had.

Atwood provides a character foil to Anne-Marie in the form of Felix's imagined daughter. Felix imagines his daughter, Miranda, at the age she would have been had she not died of meningitis. This character slowly becomes real for the reader, taking on characteristics as she learns advanced maths, plays chess with Felix and sings outside his window. Felix imagines her eating dinner with him and going through phases of eating healthy food like quinoa as he imagines what a young girl would be like. She lives a sheltered life in the cottage and when she finally travels to the prison he has to explain what a car is before she will travel in it. Her decision to be Ariel's understudy is a reminder that she is invisible to everyone but the audience and the protagonist. Through this character, Atwood creates a portrait of an ideal daughter. The fact that she only exists in Felix's imagination is a reminder that women who are completely virtuous and controlled in this manner do not exist in this world. The constant comparisons to the very real Anne-Marie give an indication of what Miranda may have been like if she had lived.

The final woman who is important in Felix's life is Estelle. She has hired him for the role as teacher and knows immediately who he is. She keeps his secrets and enables him to achieve his plan. She often pulls strings with the Board, helping Felix to get Anne-Marie into the prison and to separate the politicians from the other dignitaries to watch *The Tempest*. In this way she is performing some of the functions of the guiding star who brought Prospero to the island, and some of Ariel, as she is helping him to manipulate his environment and enact the plot. She is also a desirable woman. Felix indicates that there is some interest between them and that this could develop further.

Quote

> "That foul mouth of hers had always startled him. He was never ready when a slice of filth came out of her child-like mouth."
>
> (Felix's reflection on Anne-Marie) Page 97

Textual Conversations about Women

Through her re-envisioning of Miranda, Atwood is implying that the characterisation of Prospero's daughter was too perfect and is thus unattainable. Through contrasting the real and the imagined characters, Atwood is implying that such idealised perfection only lives in the imagination and that real women have more agency and are multi-faceted. Felix's shock or discomfort when Ann-Marie is not innocent or vulnerable is a reminder of the third wave of feminism and the opportunities women now have. Through developing several characters, Atwood is revealing that different women of differing status and age have the ability to speak and be heard. The fact that Estelle is a crucial element in Felix's success is further evidence of the changing values and contexts of the texts.

Gonzalo in *The Tempest*

Gonzalo is the adviser of Alonso the King of Naples in *The Tempest*. Though he is technically a part of the plot to usurp Prospero, he is solely responsible for Prospero and Miranda's survival as he has stowed food and water away on their boat when they are set adrift. He also hides Prospero's magic books aboard the boat, so he clearly does not have any religious qualms about the study of the dark arts, or he does not understand what they are, which is perhaps more likely. Due to the kindness shown to Prospero, his life is spared when it is threatened by Antonio and Sebastian.

One of the great ironies in this characterisation is the fact that the adviser is not particularly intelligent, and Gonzalo often lacks the education of the nobles around him. He optimistically puts forward a vision for his rule of the island, referencing More's *Utopia* for the audience, but he contradicts himself whilst outlining the rules for his kingdom. He also gets mythological references wrong, a fact pointed out by his critics, Sebastian and Antonio.

Lonnie in *Hag-Seed*

As the Chairman of the Makeshiweg Festival Board, Lonnie has been part of the plan to oust Felix when he is still grieving over his daughter. Yet his regret is evident in his attempt to apologise to Felix. He is responsible for giving Felix his annotated script of *The Tempest* and his cape made from stuffed animal skin that he later uses to play Prospero in the prison.

At the prison, Felix spares Lonnie, ensuring that he doesn't eat the grapes which are laced with the drugs. His benevolent nature is also obvious when he is the first to suggest that what they have experienced was just theatre.

Textual Conversations about Gonzalo

Atwood removes the comic aspects of Gonzalo's character when she reimagines him, focusing more on his benevolent and optimistic nature in her portrayal of Lonnie. While there is some theatricality in his exaggerated gestures, like the flowers he throws on Miranda's grave, due to the new form, the more realistic postmodern novel, the comic aspects of the play are no longer relevant. His character does still function to reveal the protagonist's humanity and to show that Felix does not want people who have been kind to him to suffer needlessly.

Antonio in *The Tempest*

Prospero's brother and the new Duke of Milan, Antonio is the reason that Prospero and Miranda have been cast out to sea and end up on the island. Their past is revealed in the backstory that Prospero tells his daughter, explaining that he let Antonio deal with the affairs of the state whilst he became increasingly involved with studying the dark arts. Antonio has given Alonso, as the sovereign of Naples, power over Milan in return for his help usurping his brother and removing him from power. The fact that both the three-year-old Miranda and Prospero should have perished at sea shows how ruthless his plan was.

Antonio is given an opportunity to reveal his Machiavellian character for the audience when Ariel leaves him awake with Sebastian whilst the rest of the nobles are sleeping. His plan to murder Alonso, who has given him power, shows his lack of loyalty and his deceitful nature. His lies and consistent jeers make him an unlikeable character. However, there is no clear justice for Antonio's sins. Prospero does not reveal his deception in the course of the play.

Quote

> "O, that you bore
> The mind that I do! What a sleep were this
> For your advancement!"
>
> (Antonio to Sebastian) II, i, 263–265

Tony Price in *Hag-Seed*

The clear villain in the novel, Tony Price convinced the board of the Makeshiweg Theatre Festival to terminate Felix's contract and to make Tony the Artistic Director instead. Tony took advantage of Felix's grief to make him seem irrational and as he had taken over all of Felix's administrative duties by that point, it seems an easy task to sway the Board in Tony's favour. As the novel is told in third person limited narration, Felix's perspective of the event is shown as he recalls it with great wrath.

Tony uses the festival as a starting point for his career, beginning a career as a politician quickly after this event. He attends the prison with the political party and is quickly caught up in what he believes is a riot. When Sal and Lonnie are asleep, Tony tries to convince Sebert that they should kill them and blame it on the prisoners. This plan, in the setting of the prison, reminds you that they are much more dangerous and less noble than the prisoners who initially scared them.

Quote

> "Let me spell it out," says Tony. "A couple of hundred years ago we would take advantage of the chaos and dispose of Sal, and blame it on the rioters."
>
> Page 221

Textual Conversations about Antonio

Atwood has faithfully reconstructed the villain in her novel. In both, the character is initially viewed through the perspective of the protagonist and the language conveys the extreme injury done to the main character, psychologically and in terms of their position. In the play and the novel, this is followed by a scene where the audience can then witness the character's actions for themselves, and their murderous intent reveals their true disloyalty and deception.

Alonso and Ferdinand in *The Tempest*

Alonso is the King of Naples. He has made a deal with Antonio for power over Milan, in return for using Naples' troops to help get Prospero out of power and give Antonio the throne. While he has previously made this deal, he readily accepts Prospero's forgiveness and daughter. Perhaps due to the suffering he has undergone, Alonso is ready to accept Prospero as an equal and start a new future with their children united.

Alonso was travelling because his daughter Claribel was marrying the King of Tunisia. Alonso appears to grieve for her loss as well as for the loss of Ferdinand. The loss of his son weighs on Alonso greatly, and he is clearly a loving and doting father. He easily accepts Miranda as his daughter-in-law as this is the choice that his son has made.

The Prince of Naples, Ferdinand believes that he has become King when he thinks he is the sole survivor from the ship. Despite this status, he accepts Prospero's power over him fairly quickly as he desires to stay close to Miranda, indicating his romantic nature.

Both the King and the Prince help the Jacobean audience to recognise that the island is a realm of chaos. When their authority is questioned on the boat it reveals that anarchy is now reigning. When Ferdinand is completing menial labour, it shows that the proper laws of status and nobility have ceased to function on the island. In the final scenes, the Prince Ferdinand kneels to his father, reminding the audience of his recognition of his father's throne. Their authority is evident in the way they speak and the fact that serving classes now acknowledge their power again.

Quote

> "Hear my soul speak
> The very instant that I saw you, did
> My heart fly to your service."
>
> (Ferdinand to Miranda) III, i, 65–67

Sal O'Nally and Frederick in *Hag-Seed*

The heritage minister and an old school rival of Felix, Sal has agreed to the termination of Felix's contract. Felix obviously believes that Sal has some loyalty to him, as he was going to complain to him before Tony revealed that Sal had agreed to his termination. It is this alliance that Sal has made with Tony which later makes him a target for Felix's plan. When he becomes the justice minister and plans to cancel the Fletcher Correctional Players, this helps Felix to justify his plot to the prisoners.

There is some irony in the fact that Sal is a heritage minister and yet he does not see the value in Shakespeare. He prefers musicals and wants the festival to put on fewer versions of the Bard's work. In contrast, his son values theatre and Shakespeare and wants to avoid politics and the law career planned for him and move into the theatre. Frederick becomes a living part of the play and a reference to *The Tempest's* play within a play when he is forced to read Ferdinand's lines with Anne-Marie. His final role, as the assistant director for the Makeshiweg Festival reveals that he has taken over Felix's role and with Anne-Marie, is the next generation who will produce theatre.

Quote

> "Freddie says, "Dad, I'd like you to meet my new partner, Anne-Marie Greenland."
>
> Page 236

Textual Conversations about the King and Prince of Naples

In both texts, the character who represents the King has significantly betrayed the protagonist and thus becomes an integral part of his plot for vengeance. In each, he is made aware of his vulnerability through the chaos that the protagonist engineers, but his primary issue is the welfare of his son. In each text, the son represents the new generation who indicates that there is hope for the future. Both Ferdinand and Frederick reveal some misogynistic characteristics, with Ferdinand cheating at chess and speaking for his wife in public. Freddie assumes that he can form a business partnership with Anne-Marie without her consent. Atwood allows her heroine to speak openly about her opinion amongst the politicians, showing that there is a chance that Freddie and Sal will acknowledge her ideas.

Caliban in *The Tempest*

Caliban was on the island before Prospero and Miranda. A child of the Algerian witch who was left on the island and later died, Caliban is often seen as a symbol of colonial attitudes in Jacobian times. He has welcomed Prospero to the island and shown him how to survive on the isle. After attempting to rape Miranda as he wanted to create a race of his own, he has been cast into a servant's role and suffers in servitude. He resents Prospero for this treatment, which is evident from his soliloquy when he discusses the spirits which torment him.

When Caliban meets Stephano and Trinculo, he tries to convince them to kill Prospero and help him to take over the island. Choosing Stephano as the person to pledge his allegiance to indicates that he does not recognise the qualities of leadership and is misguided. When his plan fails, he is miserable as he knows that Prospero will punish him.

Caliban is referred to as being malformed. This could be seen literally, or as a reference to his exotic heritage. Several of the Italian characters who meet him recognise that they would be able to exhibit him in England for money, due to the Jacobean's obsession with viewing the exotic and oddities. The fact that they force him to drink alcohol is a reminder of the vices that colonials brought to native lands. It is also interesting to note that Caliban is more educated than both Trinculo and Stephano, as he is able to speak in blank verse, which is often reserved for the nobility. This is a reminder of the education Prospero gave him and of his own worth.

Quote

> "Sometime am I
> All wound with adders, who with cloven tongues
> Do hiss me into madness."
>
> (Caliban about Prospero's punishments) II, ii, 12–14

Representations of Caliban in Hag-Seed

Atwood does not give the reader one central figure whom they can identify as Caliban, despite calling the book *Hag-Seed*, one of the derogatory names used for Caliban. Yet, there is an argument that the prisoners represent Caliban in the novel. This can be seen as the men exist in the prison, the isolated location, before Felix arrives. He also envisages that they may be a threat to Anne-Marie and ensures that he shows them a video of her physical dancing to try to protect her from advances. Felix educates them as their teacher, teaching them about a culture that has little relevance to their lives, just as Prospero does to Caliban.

Fifteen of the prisoners want to play Caliban in the play, as they feel that he is like him. They understand the circumstance that he is in and the fact that he wants vengeance for it. Leggs ultimately achieves the part and delivers a rap which states that he will violently murder Prospero and keep Miranda as his sex slave. Leggs' conviction is PTSD related as he is a war veteran and had addiction issues. This indicates that his incarceration is due to factors spiralling out of control and draws parallels with Caliban.

Quote

> "'We *get* him.'
>
> 'Everyone kicks him around but he doesn't let it break him, he says what he thinks.' This from Leggs."
>
> (The prisoners discussing Caliban.) Page 120

Textual Conversations about Caliban

Atwood has referenced the importance of Caliban in the title, whilst not giving him a clear counterpart in the novel. This indicates that attitudes have changed in society and that the prejudicial beliefs about native people in foreign lands are no longer acceptable or relevant for contemporary audiences. By referencing the prisoners, Atwood is introducing a new, more relevant prejudice, one that readers may themselves have whilst reading. She is pointing out the prejudice against those who are incarcerated, arguing against the belief that they cannot be re-educated and therefore framing the character in a more relevant context.

Sebastian in *The Tempest*

The brother of the King of Naples, Sebastian is convinced by Antonio that he should take advantage of the shipwreck to seize the crown. His intent to murder his brother reveals his lack of religious values and the evil within him.

He is often seen in conversation with Antonio and their bond is evident. Many of their interactions involve making fun of Gonzalo or proving his own wit.

Sebert in Hag-Seed

Sebert is running against Sal O'Nally in the polls and attends the prison with Tony. He obviously has a bond with Tony, similar to that seen in the play. He is also convinced to kill his rival in order to take power. In both, the protagonist threatens him with disclosing his murderous plot, but it is not yet revealed and may never be.

Trinculo and Stephano in *The Tempest*

These characters are comic characters in the play and mainly intended to amuse the audience. They are both from the serving class, Trinculo is a jester and Stephano is a butler. The fact that the butler is now drinking the wine that he would usually be serving to the nobles would be amusing for the audience.

When Caliban acknowledges them as his new masters, the audience would recognise that he does not understand what nobility and leadership look like. Their inability to execute the plan and the fact that they are distracted by the fine clothes laid out is a reminder to the Jacobean audience that the lower class is not fit to lead and thus looks ridiculous in these noble garments.

Comic or equivalent characters in *Hag-Seed*

While Atwood does not create characters who are the exact equivalent to Stephano and Trinculo, she does utilise a range of comic incidents which use high or low culture to create comedy. The use of the Shakespearean curses in the prisoner's dialogue makes the dialogue comic, particularly as it references the high culture not usually associated with prisons. The raps, dances and costumes of the Fletcher Correctional Players also mix high and low culture to comic effect and often offer light relief, performing the same function as the clowns in the original play.

Quote

> "It was my bro called Prospero"
>
> (From SnakeEye's rap about Antonio) page 156

Activities for Characters

- Choose one pair of characters. Write a list of five of their qualities, or characteristics. (For example, Miranda might be innocent, romantic etc.) For each element on this list, find one quote to prove that quality or characteristic. Do this for each text.
- Looking through this character list, what conscious changes can you see that Atwood has made? List them. Then take one of these changes and explore why Atwood may have done this, with reference to both texts and contexts.

Resonances and Dissonances in Setting

The Tempest is set wholly on the secluded island that has been home to Prospero and Miranda for the past twelve years. The island is primitive and almost deserted when they arrive and Caliban is the only human resident. As an anagram of the word cannibal in its original spelling, Caliban's name insinuates that he is a wild native in an exotic location. Yet his initial benevolence is indicated by the fact that he teaches Miranda and Prospero how to find water and feed themselves on the island.

Prospero has attempted to civilise the island, evidenced by the cell he has to sleep in, where Miranda and Ferdinand are found playing chess. He has instituted a servant class, utilising Caliban as his servant to fetch wood and conduct menial tasks. Through his interactions with Miranda, it is evident that he has established the patriarchal norms of Europe.

Travelling between Tunisia and Italy, the nobles are shipwrecked on the same island, indicating the location of the island. Ariel is able to hide their ship in a harbour and divide the nobles easily, tiring them out by making them walk around, indicating the size of the land mass.

Through Prospero's backstory and through the staging of the nobles on the island, references to the civilised Italian setting are continually made. The anarchy of the island is established in the first scene, when the status of the nobles is not recognised. The continual mistreatment of the nobles reminds the audience of the primitive anarchy of the island setting.

Atwood does not create a setting that is a tabula rasa, or blank slate, as Shakespeare's island was. Instead she locates her story within contemporary society which has the cultural and social paradigms of the existing world embedded within it.

Felix's story is mainly set in Ontario, Canada. The town of Makeshiweg (a fictional town, whose name means fox in a Canadian Indigenous language) is the equivalent of Milan. The town represents culture and privilege, as this is where the theatre festival is held.

Once Felix is fired, he flees to Atwood's version of the island, which takes a few forms. He finds a shack located on the farmland of a surly couple, Maude and Bert. The basic dwelling has only two rooms and an outhouse, allowing for the primitive seclusion which is similar to that which Prospero endured.

The prison is the second location that mimics the island in the novel. It imprisons the characters, particularly if you take the view that the prisoners represent Caliban, who never leaves Prospero's island. The guards, like the spirits of the island, keep the prisoners contained. The prison setting has several classrooms that they use to film their video scenes in. This allows them to separate the politicians later and create the anarchic interactive theatre experience which replicates *The Tempest*.

One dissonant element is the wide variety of locations that Atwood utilises in telling Felix's story. In the course of the novel he visits various locations in Toronto and Wilmot. He moves from toy stores to costume shops and from burger joints to expensive restaurants, showing his versatility. He also uses the internet to spy on his enemies from a distance, reminding the audience of the technological zeitgeist of the era.

Activities for Setting

- What is one setting that Atwood has mimicked closely? Explain how she has done this and why.
- Choose two contemporary locations and explain why they have been included, in your opinion.

Language Features, Narrative Techniques and other Devices

Shakespeare and Atwood have both created texts that use forms and features in traditional and unique ways. The composers had individually had a history of success in their medium and thus each have the ability to experiment in the form that they know so well.

Shakespeare had written primarily in three genres of plays: tragedy, comedy and history. Yet with *The Tempest* he melded elements of tragedy and comedy to invent the tragicomedy genre, something unknown to his audience. He presented a hero whose obsession with magic and revenge made him blinkered and could have led to his downfall, yet he is allowed the happy ending, overseeing the marriage that ends every comedy play. The play further has elements of revenge tragedy exhibited and also has some historical basis in the recent shipwrecks like the *Sea Venture*.

The play does have some traditional elements. Like all Shakespearian plays, it has a five act structure. However, the placement of an epilogue was something not often seen in Shakespeare's work. In this play he additionally used Aristotle's unities for theatre, setting the play in one place, making the action happen in one day and arguably only having one plot.

The play is written in iambic pentameter, with the structured lines of blank verse being used to indicate civility and nobility. Prospero has clearly educated Caliban and Miranda, as they both speak in iambic pentameter, even when delivering soliloquies. However, when the servants Trinculo and Stephano appear, they speak in prose, the insinuation being that they lack the nobility to rule and are not as worthy or educated as Caliban or Miranda.

The influence of the Renaissance is evident in the allusions interwoven throughout the play, with mythological and historical allusion to ancient Greek and Roman culture embedded throughout. References to Dido, Juno, Cupid and the harpy all rely on an educated audience to ensure that they are fully understood. The use of the masque within the play and the antimasque before this, additionally incorporates Renaissance concepts. The masque was an innovation of Renaissance court, where masked actors represented allegorical figures to show concepts of peace and harmony. Usually, clowns were hired to create chaos and disorder before the graceful masked figures provided order. The masque was essentially a representation of the power of the monarchy and its addition reveals the influence of King James on the writing and production of the play.

Other staging decisions reveal Shakespeare's innovation and movement away from his normal lack of direction. He specified actions for many of his characters. Miranda sleeps and begs on her knees, Ferdinand is frozen with his sword drawn and Ariel is invisible, though we can see him. Prospero wears a magic cloak, carries a staff and has a magic book, all props that become symbolic when he personifies them when deciding to "drown" them. Additionally, there are music and songs which add to the atmosphere of wonder and help to entertain the audience. Atwood tried to include many of these stage techniques in her novel, referencing the props and costumes in the story and including the raps and dances to show the theatricality of the production.

The soliloquies and staging of Prospero are used to showcase his anguish and later his growing empathy. He is often unobserved onstage, such as when he watches Miranda and Ferdinand interact, implying his manipulation. Atwood uses different means to show a manipulative and multilayered character. Her narration is third person but written as free indirect discourse, meaning that it is focalised on the protagonist, allowing the reader to understand his inner thoughts. His control of the politicians and environment is done through technology and illegal drugs, giving the text realism whilst still invoking the moral issues explored in the original.

The motifs of the original play include a focus on sleep and waking, imagery that centers on water and the heavens, and a wider focus on nature. Whilst the sleep motif is not as prevalent, the natural motif is evident throughout the novel. Felix often uses it when he discusses Miranda, perhaps to insinuate that this is a natural reaction to his grief (or an unnatural one perhaps.) The celestial imagery is evoked often in the passages for Estelle, reminding audiences that she might be a physical manifestation of the guiding star that brought the wayward travellers to the island. The motif of water is prominent in the end of the novel, where its traditional symbolism as a sign of healing is used for Felix as he plans to cruise away to his future.

Atwood is not writing a realist novel, but a postmodern text. The novel is a reimagining of a known work, with a hybridised style and an unusual pastiche of forms. It begins with a script, moves into prose and incorporates lists and rap into its form. The linear timeline is disrupted and from the beginning the dialogue and prose is shocking and challenges expected conventions. The narrator is questionable, exhibited when Miranda's voice is able to be heard by a third party, which makes us question whether she exists. The question of whether a character like Miranda, made up by another character, is more or less real than the delusionary character is a paradoxical idea in itself. Plus, the novel incorporates elements of the multiverse when Felix allows the prisoners to envision differing futures for *The Tempest*'s characters. Obviously, the novel is postmodern and includes many innovative elements in its form.

The concept of metafiction may not be wholly innovative, but the influence of the original text. The fact that Atwood includes a play within her novel reflects *The Tempest*'s play within the play. This metafictional element makes the audience question the role of the composer and their own role as the audience. There are further metafictive features in the original play. Prospero's initial address to his daughter to hear his tale is often read as an address to the audience. The epilogue comments that Prospero is caught in the world of the island forever and can only be freed by the applause of the audience. The fourth wall is clearly being broken in these scenes.

While Atwood's creative use of form is often ingenious, she is reflecting the innovation of Shakespeare with many of her features. Undoubtably the most unusual and creative of her own unique elements was the female character foils of Miranda and Anne-Marie. By creating a character who is wholly imagined by the protagonist, manifested by grief and symbolic of dying patriarchal norms, Atwood questions both the play, our society and what we believe about fiction itself.

Activity

- Write out three techniques that are used by both Atwood and Shakespeare. Include quotes or examples and explain how the techniques are used in each text. Link each to the values they reflect in society.

Textual Conversations

This unit requires you to compare texts and the similarities and differences between them. These resonances and dissonances can be seen in many different aspects of the texts. Some of the aspects that you might discuss, so that you can develop your personal perspective of the texts are:

- The themes, or issues of the texts are one way that you can connect them. The themes such as power, desire for human connection, order and chaos, status and the other all appear in both texts. *(Check the themes section of this book as each theme is discussed separately.)*
- The portrayal of Prospero, his fall from a position of power, his imprisonment and anger and his final acceptance and healing are shown in both texts. *(Check the Characters section of this book as Prospero and his representation and journey from power is discussed in detail.)*
- The other characters of the texts are one way that you can connect them. The major characters like Miranda, versions of Ariel and Antonio appear in each text. *(Check the Characters section of this book as each character is discussed in each text and the connections made between their portrayals are discussed afterwards.)*
- The structure of the texts is similar. Both texts follow Shakespeare's original structure of starting in the chaos of the tempest, delving into the backstory and charting the path of the protagonist's plan, whilst the contemporary audience's attention is kept by the constant diversions in Atwood's more innovative structure.
- Both align in "presenting the plot of revenge." The forms and features used to show the protagonist's revenge do differ. Shakespeare used the traditional Aristotelian unities and the play form, whilst Atwood's use of focalisation on Felix and interior monologue makes the path of his vengeance and redemption more a personal drama.
- Shakespeare's audience were viewing a play with a highly inventive hybrid genre, unusual characters and a creative plot. They would be used to knowing the basic story of the play before they went

to the theatre, so this lack of knowledge would be new to them. However, Atwood's audience would often have a solid foundation of knowledge of *The Tempest* to begin the novel. Yet her inventive changes and settings would be surprising to her readers.

- Foreshadowing is used in the play and the novel. Both texts forewarn the audience constantly, predicting what will occur and what Prospero will do. Shakespeare does this in soliloquies, Atwood in her dialogue and narration.
- Both texts glorify Shakespeare's theatre and art. *The Tempest* has many metatheatrical elements like the masque and the epilogue to help the audience consider the role of the theatre and the director. The subtext of the novel is the transformative power of Shakespeare and his plays, shown through the role they have in the lives of Felix, Anne-Marie and the prisoners.
- The texts have a divergent view of Caliban's deformity and origin. Shakespeare presents this in a manner that reflects colonial attitudes, revealing the prejudice towards those of different races and origins to the Europeans. Atwood highlights the racism inherent in the text through the prisoner's discussions. She further reminds readers of their own prejudices about inmates through their assumptions regarding characters in the novel.
- Both texts use music and humour to entertain their audience. Shakespeare uses music through the masque and Ariel and the slapstick comedy of Trinculo and Stephano who are the clowns of the play. Atwood replicates this through the raps and dances of the prisoners. The performances are often deliberately ridiculous and humorous, the dances and songs adding an entertaining element.
- *The Tempest* displays the lack of status women have in their society through the roles of women, particularly in the lack of women onstage. Atwood rectifies this with three strong female characters but includes one who is merely a mirage to remind audiences of the lack of feminism within the initial text.

Activities

1. Use a mind map to represent the three aspects where the composers have shown the most prominent convergence of opinion or ideas and the three points where they have distinctly diverged in their manner of presenting an aspect to the audience. For each, write one sophisticated sentence that introduces the connection that exists between the texts. Then add a reference to two scenes, two quotes and four techniques that illustrate this connection. In another colour, explain how the representation of this connection reflects the composer's values, assumptions or perspectives.
2. Brainstorm as many links and similarities between the texts that you can think of. Now draw up a table, with "Explicit link" on one side and "Implicit link" on the other. Decide whether you think each connection or link is explicit or implicit. Once you have finished, choose one link from each list. Explain how these links have helped you to understand the values, assumptions or perspectives and the significance and context of each text.

The Essay

The essay has been the subject of numerous texts and you should have the basic form well in hand. As teachers, the point we would emphasise would be to link the paragraphs both to each other and back to your argument (which should directly respond to the question). Of course, ensure your argument is logical and sustained.

Make sure you use specific examples and that your quotes are accurate. To ensure that you respond to the question make sure you plan carefully and are sure what relevant point each paragraph is making. It is solid technique to actually 'tie up' each point by explicitly coming back to the question.

When composing an essay the basic conventions of the form are:

- **State your argument, name the texts, outline the points to be addressed.**

↓

A solid structure for each paragraph is:

- **Topic sentence** ***(the main idea and its link to the previous paragraph/argument)***
- **Explanation / discussion of the point including links between texts if applicable.**
- **Detailed evidence** ***(Close textual reference- quotes, incidents and technique discussion.)***
- **Tie up by restating the point's relevance to argument / question**

↓

- **Summary of points**
- **Final sentence that restates your argument**

As well as this basic structure you will need to focus on:

Audience – for the essay the audience must be considered formal unless specifically stated otherwise. Therefore, your language must reflect the audience. This gives you the opportunity to use the jargon and vocabulary that you have learnt in English. For the audience ensure your introduction is clear and has impact. Avoid slang or colloquial language including contractions (like, doesn't, e.g., etc.).

Purpose – the purpose of the essay is to answer the question given. The examiner evaluates how well you can construct an argument and understand the module's issues and its text(s). An essay is solidly structured so its composer can analyse ideas. This is where you earn marks. It does not retell the story or state the obvious.

Communication – Take a few minutes to plan the essay. If you rush into your answer it is almost certain you will not make the most of the brief 40 minutes you have to show all you know about the question. More likely you will include irrelevant details that do not gain you marks but waste your precious time. Remember an essay is formal so do not do the following: story-tell, list and number points, misquote, use slang or colloquial language, be vague, use non sentences or fail to address the question.

Writing Points for a Textual Conversations Essay

This can be a hard module to respond to, as the syllabus requires you to include a number of things in your response. No matter what type of question you are given, try to ensure that for EACH POINT you make you have covered these aspects:

- You should be clear whether this point resonates or is dissonant in the two texts.
- You must display your knowledge of the play *The Tempest*, and the dominant ideas that are relevant for the question.
- Your answer should reveal the depth of your knowledge by including quotes, examples and techniques from the play.
- You must make a reference to the contextual aspects that have influenced this part of the play.
- You need to try and discuss the values and assumptions in the text that reflect Shakespeare's context.
- You must display your knowledge of the novel *Hag-Seed*, and the dominant ideas that are relevant for the question.
- Your answer should reveal the depth of your knowledge by including quotes, examples and techniques from the novel.
- You must make a reference to the contextual aspects that have influenced this part of the novel.
- You need to try and discuss the values, assumptions and perspectives in the text that reflect this contemporary context and how they clash or align with the original text.
- You must connect the two texts, and discuss how and why changes occurred.
- You should be considering your own values and assumptions and developing your own theories and opinions about the texts.

If you are unsure how to include all of these varied aspects in one essay, look carefully at the model essay presented in this guide.

Structuring an Essay Response

Read carefully the question below and then examine the essay outline on the following pages. Try to develop your essay along these lines and also develop strategies to answer questions that are not essay based.

A list of these response types is given at the end of the sample essay. Look at these and ensure you become familiar with most of them. Try to practise them when you can and develop your writing skills.

It is worthwhile looking back at the rubric for Module A, as many of the keywords in essay questions are directly or indirectly (i.e. through synonyms) sourced from there.

The model essay that follows requires you to focus on particular elements highlighted in the keywords of the question. Spend a few moments working out what these keywords are, so you can link to them effectively.

Question

> "Ideas which resonate between texts often allow further insight into both the original and the reimagined work."

Discuss the ideas which resonate between *The Tempest* and *Hag-Seed* and how studying them in tandem can enhance the audience's understanding of both texts.

(Try to answer this question. A sample introduction and some planning notes are written for you. Read the sample essay first.)

A few notes about answering this question:

- Never forget that this is the module where you must discuss context and comparisons. Even if the question does not specifically discuss context, your essay should refer to some of the influences on the texts. Ensure that your references to context or influences are appropriate to the points you are making. You should never be writing out the whole history of the context without linking it to a viable argument.

- Good essays have a thesis, a line of argument that is valid and answers the question. Examiners will look for this thesis when marking you and determining your grade.
- You will need to determine what the ideas are that the texts present. Ideas could be concepts, the themes, the presentations of characters, the action in the text or the purpose of the work.
- There are more ideas in the texts than you could ever cover, so choose those ideas that you know you can discuss in an impressive, intelligent way.
- In an open question, try to balance the information that you give. Don't do all themes, or all characters or you will look like it's all you know. A good essay might focus on one or two concepts, plus one or two characters and perhaps a reference to the purpose or form of the text.
- Ensure that you balance the texts in your essay. You should not have more on either text. You want to come across as someone who understands them both.
- You need to ensure that you are actively making connections between the texts. A good essay won't just discuss how the play sheds light on the novel, but will make reference to times when the novel allows insight into the play.
- Whilst you will be busy connecting the texts and referring to context, you cannot forget that you need to reveal your depth of understanding of each text. You will need quotes and techniques for each text. Do not ignore the novel's techniques; they are just as important as Shakespeare's devices.
- You do not have to discuss the play first, just because it was written before the novel. It is just as viable to discuss the novel first, and this can make your essay stand out from the others.

Sample Essay Response

Question

> "Reinventing texts is a way to display the shifting power dynamics of our world."

To what extent is this true of *The Tempest* and *Hag-Seed* when viewed in conjunction?

Response:

Power and status define an individual's place in the world, determining their experience and privilege. Significant texts function to reflect the paradigms of power in society, revealing shifting patterns of privilege. Shakespeare's Renaissance tragicomedy *The Tempest* revealed inequity and chaos caused by power shifts which would have caused the Jacobean audience to question contextual concepts of power. When reimagining this world in *Hag-Seed*, Atwood undoubtedly furthers this questioning from a postmodern, postcolonial lens. Whilst continuing to investigate the effect of political manoeuvring and the inequity of the prejudicial treatment of Caliban, Atwood consistently highlights the patriarchal structures inherent in the key text. Her revision calls for readers to question the assumptions that privilege characters and their fates in the original, as well as those structures represented in her reimagined text.

The Tempest aims to highlight shifting power structures and reinforce the place of the court and the king. The influence of King James is highly apparent in the characterisation of Prospero, who has been usurped by Antonio and Alonso. Reflecting the Gunpowder Plot and the recent execution of Guy Fawkes, audiences would recognise the evil characterisation of Antonio as being emblematic of the world which had threatened their king. His belittling, betting and the condescending tone he levels at the pure heated Gonzalo, are consistent evidence of his villainy. Antonio's status as the new Duke of Milan is a disruption to the power structures determined by birth order. The chaos of the titular tempest, which forces the nobles aboard the tumultuous vessel to acquiesce to the threatening boatswain, symbolically forcing them to retreat underneath him to a lower deck, highlights the result when the Chain of Being has been subverted. As the Machiavellian Antonio has power instead of Prospero, harmony cannot be restored in this world. The later use of the masque represents that order will be restored and foreshadows the peace possible when the correct authority figure is able to rule. Iris in the masque symbolises harmony and Ceres, fertility, indicating that through Miranda's progeny, Prospero's line will again rule Milan and also Naples. Through his play, Shakespeare is confirming the Jacobean belief that power is conferred on those who are born to rule and that altering power structures is disruptive and evil.

Hag-Seed revises the protagonist's struggle for power to reveal changing attitudes to status. Felix has fallen from a position as an artistic director of a well-known theatre company that experiences "triumphs with the critics" to a recluse living in a secluded hovel. Atwood's revisions change Antonio to Tony, a self-serving politician who "swills champagne", "attends galas" and becomes the Minister for Heritage. Probably reflecting international politicians like Trump and May, the characterisation is both humorous and ironic, as it is a stereotype of the upper class and an ironic comment that those in charge of heritage despise Shakespeare and prefer musicals. In this portrayal of power broking, the manoeuvring is still occurring on a political level, however, the effect is no longer seen as cataclysmic. Instead, it affects only individuals. Felix's inner monologue reveals his anger at his fall from power, anaphorically stating that

> "It rankles. It festers. It brews vengefulness…"

His metaphorical references to afflictions and potions remind readers of the supernatural powers Prospero possessed that this impotent Felix lacks. His response to his fall from grace is self-imposed exile. The setting of the rural cabin is reminding the audience that individuals often cannot cope with losing status and privilege in the modern world. The result when an individual loses power is mental illness, as portrayed by Felix's gradual slide into insanity. There is also a commentary here about the lack of mental health systems for those with no access to health care in Canada. Just like Prospero, Atwood isolates Felix, making his decisions more and more deranged. This then highlights the fact that Shakespeare is also revealing a similar concept in his play. Chaos and disorder is not just occurring on a macular level, but within the microcosm of Prospero's world. He is clearly becoming less rational as he talks to spirits, immerses himself in magic and displays his power in disappearing feasts and harpies. Thus the revision definitively shows us that it is important to focus on the disorder and anguish in the protagonist's mind which results in a loss of power for the ruling class, and not just that which occurred in the wider world.

Atwood's commentary that losing power after a time of privilege causes distress and anguish allows readers to examine *The Tempest* with a new lens. It is not just the protagonist who has fallen from grace, but Caliban who has lost his position in his social circle. As the Algerian son of Sycorax and the first inhabitant of the island, Caliban's name as an anagram of the old English spelling of cannibal represents the indigenous people who suffered under European Imperialism. Caliban's anger at his position is driven by the fact that he was previously seen as equal to Prospero and Miranda, before his assumption that he could be her mate has horrified the Italian pair. His soliloquy as he reveals the daily torture by Prospero uses cumulative listing to impress upon the listener the many physical torments he faces since becoming a slave. Yet the iambic pentameter indicates his worth as owner of the isle, particularly when later juxtaposed with the prose of servants Trinculo and Stephano. Shakespeare is challenging the Jacobean audience's colonial attitudes through these lines, indicating that their assumptions about power and privilege may be incorrect. While Atwood's portrayal of the suffering individuals face after losing power, reminds the reader on reflection that Caliban would feel even more keenly his lack of power, after having previously been given a position of privilege. When viewed in conjunction, Caliban's suffering on the island due to his fall from power is apparent.

Hag-Seed astutely comments on the shifting power dynamics of race and prejudice in the world since the play has first been shown. The prisoners react to Caliban's portrayal, seizing upon the slave's otherness as the reason for his poor treatment. Prospero has labelled Caliban a "thing of darkness" and this metaphor can be seen as a reference to both his skin as well as his actions in trying to gain power. In the prisoner's multiverse of the characters' future, many believe that Caliban will be saved from the island, but only so that he can be exhibited as a souvenir of savagery. They are indicating that even though Prospero has acknowledged that Caliban is his creature, that the colonial prejudices of the Jacobeans will never allow Caliban status.

The modern world has fewer prejudices, which is evident in the 2016 novel. Caliban is seen as a status symbol for the prisoners and fifteen of them want to play the character, and appear on the video that will be viewed by the rest of the inmates and shown to the visiting ministers. It is Caliban's status as the other which connects the prisoners to the Algerian slave, who is so important that he is represented in the novel's title and symbolised by every prisoner in Atwood's revision. The men state that they "get him", colloquially explaining their connection with the imprisoned slave. They glorify him as "King Hag-Seed" with raps and dances, celebrating his pain as he rages against his captor. Yet just like Caliban, the majority of these prisoners will be abandoned by the Prospero figure by the end of the play's journey and will be left without power or status. Atwood has Felix arrange a release for the computer hacker and forger 8Handz, but leaves the other men, those guilty of assault, manslaughter, defrauding senior citizens and gang violence, locked in the prison. Through their affinity with Caliban and her titular reference, Atwood is insinuating that despite our postcolonial values, there are still prejudices in 2016, especially towards the incarcerated. Those in the penal system become powerless and often never escape.

The reimagining of *The Tempest* does give some hope that a major power shift has occurred, evident in the revision of the female characters in the play. The original play only featured one of the three female characters on stage. The witch Sycorax had died long before the play began. Claribel's marriage to the King of Tunis has left her far from Naples. Only Miranda is able to represent women of her time. In the first scene her father's control of her is evident, as he forces Miranda to sit, listen and sleep on command. This staging is a reminder of the patriarchal control Prospero has over his daughter. Even in her relationship with Ferdinand when she is defying her father, he stands onstage observing, the insinuation being that Miranda has been manipulated into acting in the way he wanted. The many references to her "virgin-knot" and the importance of her being a "maid or no", which is the first question Ferdinand asks her, is a reminder that she is only of value as a potential bride and a bargaining tool to create an alliance. King James had requested this play be shown at the marriage of his own daughter Elizabeth to Frederick of Palatine. It was probably seen as an ideal play to reflect the Princess' role in creating an alliance that solidified her father's power.

Four centuries later, women are more than just bargaining tools and have power and agency themselves. Atwood reflected this through her own three female characters, all who appear and speak in the novel and have completely different characterisations. Estelle is more than just a representation of Prospero's guiding light. She is an attractive, flirtatious woman who is strong, connected and technically Felix's boss. The celestial imagery Atwood uses for her, calling her a "Star" and having them meet at a café called Zenith, highlight her power in this political arena. Another female character whose agency is evident is Anne-Marie, whose physical capacity is emphasised through her dancing. A contrast to Miranda, Anne-Marie uses her sexuality to control WonderBoy and Freddie. The power shift from patriarchal dominance to a position of power amongst men is evident for Atwood's female characters.

However, the imagined Miranda is Atwood's triumph. The author of the iconic polemic "Spotty Handed Villainesses" and the feminist speculative fiction *The Handmaid's Tale* always has an astute commentary on patriarchal politics evident in her texts, and *Hag-Seed* is no exception. The delusioned Felix imagines his daughter at different stages of her life, aging her and imaging her as the perfect young girl he wishes she was. His absolute control of her determines that she does not see his plotting and that she is only able to adopt habits and hobbies that he deems appropriate. He gifts her cooking, the ability to play chess, and advanced maths capabilities to prove that hc is a progressive father. Yet the character foil of Anne-Marie reminds the reader that Felix has little understanding of real women. He is shocked by her cursing and often upset when she challenges his decisions. Atwood is casting Felix in the role of the middle-aged man who is not progressive enough to understand shifting power dynamics in his world. His Miranda does not exist, because she cannot, she is too perfect. Considering the original play, this can be seen as a commentary on the characterisation. Atwood is perhaps challenging the authenticity of the original Miranda and questioning whether women like this really existed anywhere except in a contained space like the island setting. Therefore her characterisation can be read as commentary on shifting patriarchal norms.

However, it can be argued that the novel is commenting on fiction and the nature of creation through the depiction of Miranda. *Hag-Seed* offers a metafictive moment where the imagined Miranda's voice is heard by 8Handz through his headphones. The song he hears, "Row Row Row Your Boat" is symbolic of philosophically questioning reality and whether life is real or "but a dream". Here the reader questions whether an imagined character is any more real than the characters imagined by the author themselves. Or since she only echoes a childhood song, perhaps Atwood's Miranda is a comment on how women would be raised if they were never allowed to speak for themselves, just as Miranda stopped speaking when her new husband began talking for her in the play. However, consider that this postmodern revision reminds readers of the metatheatre within the play, where Prospero points out that they are all just "an insubstantial pageant" and shall fade leaving "not a rack behind". To an extent, the original protagonist Prospero is reminding the audience that the play within the play is like all theatre and is not worth anything, indicating that all the characters are not true representations of people. Yet the metonymic meaning of the soliloquy is that the play is just like life and will end, paving the way for the next generation, which is evidence that power dynamics shift continually as generations die. Therefore, it doesn't matter if characters are real or imagined. Art remains as a reminder of the past, and characters and their relative status and privilege can reveal the changing power dynamics of the era in which each text was created.

The reinvention of *The Tempest* focuses on a revision of patriarchal structures and results in renewed agency and power for female characters. Hag-Seed further reveals the postcolonial attitudes to the other and the fact that political manoeuvring has an individual consequence instead of being a societal matter. Through viewing the texts in conjunction, the paradigmatic shifts in power through the last four centuries are often evident.

Essay Questions

Question One

Context and values are important factors that contribute to the creation of a text. How have differing contexts and values led to the construction of different works?

Ensure that you discuss *The Tempest* and *Hag-Seed*, along with their respective contexts, values and assumptions in your answer.

Question Two

"Viewing some texts in tandem can lead to a better knowledge of each."

How has viewing *The Tempest* in conjunction with *Hag-Seed* enhanced your understanding of each text?

Question Three

"Our concept of what is evil or amoral does not essentially change."

Discuss this idea with reference to *The Tempest* and *Hag-Seed*.

Question Four

"No two texts are the same, even if they appear to be. Composers always have a different agenda. "

Evaluate this statement with reference to *The Tempest* and *Hag-Seed*.

Essay Practice

Essay Question

"Ideas which resonate between texts often allow further insight into both the original and the reimagined work."

Discuss the ideas which resonate between The Tempest *and* Hag-Seed *and how studying them in tandem can enhance the audience's understanding of both texts.*

Essay Sample Introduction

Enlightenment can be gained through studying texts in tandem, as salient ideas often resonate through similar works. When significant texts are reimagined in contemporary contexts, modern audiences often gain an insight into the original work and the reframed text, reflected through the lens of their own values and assumptions, allowing profound understanding of the concepts which are highlighted by their mirroring in each text. (Now name the two or three ideas you will focus on. They must be specifically named in the essay.)

Write the rest of this essay. (Ensure you read the notes before this, which will help you to plan the essay.)

You may need to read the sample essay which appears before this to get a sense of how to connect the two texts and how to include evidence to back up your ideas.

Other Types of Responses

It is crucial students realise that their responses in the examination, in class and in assessment tasks will NOT always be essays. This page is designed to give guidance with the different types of responses which are now required.

The response types covered in the exam may include some of the following:

- Writing reflectively
- Discursive writing
- Imaginative forms such as interview or letter.
- Speech
- Essay

Students should familiarise themselves with these types of responses and be able to write effectively in them. You should practise each one at some stage of your H.S.C. year.

Additional Questions

These questions do allow more freedom than the rigid essay writing format, but you must still conform to the confines of the set text type. You should also ensure that you are including knowledge of context, text and are exploring connections when answering this type of question.

- Write your own scene which could have been used in Atwood's novel *Hag-Seed*. Then write a reflection on how reading Atwood's work helped you to understand the style that you needed to achieve in this scene, and how your scene works as a reframing of the original play.
- You have been asked to give a speech about Textual Conversations for next year's Year Twelve students. Write this speech, ensuring that you discuss the texts that you have studied, the influences of these texts and the connections that you made.
- A new radio program entitled "Textual Conversations" is airing on your local radio station. Write the transcript for the first episode of this show, where they feature your prescribed texts.

  (Hint: You will first need to decide who your guests will be. You could use the composers, characters, historians or even students as your guests.)
- Write a feature article that might be published about your prescribed texts. The title of the article is *Textual Conversations; How Contemporary Texts are Breathing New Life into the Old.*

  Ensure that you discuss both the texts, contexts and the composers' perspectives in your answer.
- Imagine Atwood has been asked to give an interview about her novel, *Hag-Seed*, and why she thinks *The Tempest* was such an important subject. Write the transcript of this interview.

  (There are several interviews on this subject, which you may wish to read first.)
- Imagine that you were asked to keep a journal whilst you were studying the Textual Conversations unit. Write three of the entries that you might have written during the course of the unit. You

might include responses to the texts, analysis of scenes or events, reflections on the ideas that are resonant or dissonant, or your perspectives on lessons, real or imagined.

Notes